TASTING
the
PAST

TASTING
the
PAST

Recipes from the Stone Age to the Present

JACQUI WOOD

First published 2009

The History Press
The Mill, Brimscombe Port
Stroud, Gloucestershire, GL5 2QG
www.thehistorypress.co.uk

British Library Cataloguing in Publication Data.
A catalogue record for this book is available from the British Library.

ISBN 978 0 7524 4794 0

Typesetting and origination by The History Press
Printed in Great Britain

❧ Contents ❧

Introduction	6
The origins of some of our modern dietary problems	7
The Celts	9
The Romans	18
The Anglo Saxons	33
The Normans	35
The Medieval Period	44
The Elizabethans	56
The Civil War	73
The Georgians	88
The Victorians	101
The Second World War	122
The Post War Years	140
So what is British food?	154
Bibliography	156
Index	157

❧ Introduction ❧

British food has been hard to categorise in the past compared to the very distinctive cuisines of countries such as Italy, France and Germany. This is because it is an amalgamation of all of them, in the same way that the English language (the only truly European language, by the way) is a combination of five European languages: Celtic, Latin, Saxon, Viking and Norman. Our cuisine, too, is a combination of the typical foods of those that once conquered Britain over a thousand years ago.

But Britain's assimilation of the foods of other cultures did not stop after the Norman Conquest. During the Medieval period, the spices brought from the Crusades by the Normans were used in almost every dish by those who could afford them. When Britain itself began to have colonies, the culinary embellishments to our diet began again. During the Elizabethan period, strange produce coming from the New World was also adopted with relish by our forbears.

The Civil War period introduced Puritan restrictions to our daily fare, making it against the law to eat a mince pie on Christmas Day because it was thought a decadent Papist tradition. The Georgians took on chocolate and coffee with gusto and even moulded their business transactions around the partaking of such beverages. But it was really not until the Victorian period – when it was said that the sun never set on the British Empire – that our diet became truly global in nature.

This book will attempt to trace the roots of these influences on our traditional British cuisine. We should be very proud that we have adopted so much of the world's tastes into our traditional diet, rather than being ashamed of a seemingly patchwork and non-descript culinary heritage, as some people have described it.

This book will also look at the recipes we commonly use today and see if they are as modern as we think they are, or whether they have very ancient roots. I hope to show – as we cover the different periods from prehistory to the post war years right up until the 1970s – that our love affair with exotic foods is not as new a trend as some of us seem to think. I have also included some recipes that, although well used and loved throughout history, have now been completely abandoned, in the hope that a few may be revived.

This book will hopefully become a manual for those readers who want to put on a themed dinner party, providing a wide selection of recipes from each period in history. I have not included those recipes that I feel you would never want to make, as some historical cookbooks have done in the past. Instead, I want you to taste these dishes and experience what it was really like to eat during those particular periods. No one, apart from the truly adventurous among you, is going to acquire a cow's udder from the butcher and stuff it as they did in the Medieval period, or stuff a fish's stomach with chopped cod's liver!

I will begin this book by describing how our metabolism changed during the Stone Age, when we began to consume one of the most common food groups today: dairy products. Each chapter will begin with a brief introduction to the foods of the period that I found particularly fascinating during my research, and each chapter will end with the traditional Christmas food of the period (Solstice Feast food for the Celts). If you want to celebrate your Christmas in a completely different way, why not try a Roman or Norman feast?

The origins of some of our modern dietary problems

One modern phenomenon of our diet-obsessed society is the Low Carbohydrate Diet. These particular diets are thought to stem from mankind's Hunter Gatherer period, and are now designed to help those of us who have overindulged to lose weight. If one looks at any 'primitive' culture today, like the Bushmen of the Kalahari, you never see anyone overweight. The Hunter Gatherer diet comprised primarily lots of meat and fish. This type of food, once caught or hunted, would satisfy a person's hunger for longer than a cereal- or vegetable-based diet. We have all indulged in those huge Chinese takeaway meals, packed full of all sorts of vegetables that leave us feeling stuffed initially, but an hour or two later we start to feel hungry again.

As the name signifies, the hunter also gathered to supplement his protein rich diet and to add variety, although fruits and nuts would have been seasonal and most of the leaves and stems they ate were only available in the spring and summer months. To summarise, the first Stone Age diet was predominantly meat and fish with seasonal banquets of nuts, berries and vegetation. One of the few vegetables available all year round would have been seaweed, which was probably gathered at the same time that shellfish were collected from the mid shoreline. It is also true that the tastiest wild vegetables can still only be found on the shorelines of northern Europe, where most Hunter Gatherer camps are found in the archaeological digs. These tasty vegetables include such delights as Rock Samphire, Sea Beet and Sea Holly, all of which are mentioned in my previous book, *Prehistoric Cooking*.

There are, however, serious consequences today for a large percentage of the population due to the ingenuity of the first farmers. Today's generation of allergic or food intolerant people can trace the origins of their dietary problems to the culinary practices of a group of Stone Age farmers.

It has been suggested that these problems are a result of modern agricultural businessmen overproducing chemically distorted products in their desire to make it all look the same and have a long shelf life in the supermarkets. Yet one of the most common food intolerances today is wheat: a hybridised wild grass plant. To find the origins of our first attempts at hybridising plants, we have to go back to the Fertile Crescent in the Middle East 11,000 years ago, to a people known as the Natufians who gathered wild grains to make into bread. The Fertile Crescent derives its name from the abundance of not just edible wild grains and pulses, but also the ancestors of our modern domestic livestock. It was almost inevitable, therefore, that the first settlements and agricultural experiments would have begun in this particular region. The city of Jericho, which is thought to be one of the only places on the planet that has been continually occupied for 11,000 years, is where these early plant experiments started as they cross-pollinated the wild grasses of the region.

Once mankind went down the road of cultivating the land, rather than wandering over it and gathering from it, we had entered ourselves into a lifetime of drudgery tilling the earth. The term 'the daily grind' is usually associated with boring and repetitive jobs. This comes from a time when people in each settlement would have had to grind grain into flour between two stones for an hour or more each day just to produce their daily bread. Lots of bread was needed too to feed the people that had to work hard on the land to grow the grain, and so we began a cycle that has no end. So those of us that cannot tolerate the gluten rich hybridised bread wheat of today can blame those people 11,000 years ago who started our first manipulation of what was natural.

The Low Carb Diet – which is predominantly meat, fish, cheese and cream – is called the 'Hunter Gatherer Diet', as mentioned above. This description is not really accurate, though, as the hunter-gatherers did not eat any dairy products until they settled down and became farmers.

The first cultivation of cereal crops was co-dependent on the domestication of the wild bull (the auroch). These were needed to pull the primitive ploughs to cultivate the land in order to grow the crops in the first place. Large numbers of female animals were needed, and so there was always a good and constant working stock of these beasts of burden. As a consequence, there would have always been suckling calves in those settlements. It would only have taken one person to drink some of the gallons of milk those beasts produced for their calves every day to get us on the road to lactose intolerance today.

Milk is primarily designed by nature as a food for young creatures, not for adults. This group of farmers therefore began the modification of the human body to tolerate milk and milk products well into adulthood – so much so that it has became a very normal part of our northern European diet today. Those early agricultural pioneers also discovered how to make hard cheese, which was a good way to store milk protein during the winter months. 'How on earth did they discover that?' you might think.

As usual with most discoveries, it was all about circumstance and chance. The early farmers had not perfected making large ceramic pots, and so a lot of the equipment they used when they were wanderers was also used in their new settled homesteads. One piece of equipment was the calf's stomach, used to carry water and to store it in their homes. When people decided to drink milk, it was natural that they would store it in the same containers that they used for water. The calf's stomach, however, contains the enzyme rennet, with which we make our modern cheeses today. If milk was put into the calf's stomach and hung in a warm place, it would therefore turn into curds and whey, and here we have the beginnings of our worldwide cheese production.

By 4,000 BC, most of northern Europe was growing wheat and enjoying dairy products in some way or another. However, for some unknown reason this love of dairy products was only popular in *northern* Europe. If you draw a line across the top of present-day Italy and include Austria, Germany, France, Switzerland, Scandinavia and Britain, you can see those ancient 'butter border lands' today. These are the countries that still love butter with their daily bread, whereas Spain, southern Italy and a large percentage of the world's countries do not really have this tradition. The colonies, of course, took this fashion with them around the world, so there are butter-loving outposts everywhere on the globe, most notably in America. But vast areas of the planet are still lactose intolerant because they did not adapt their metabolism as the northern Europeans did so effectively during the Stone Age.

We tend to think today that the lactose intolerant person is someone whose body has rejected a good and wholesome foodstuff. It is, however, the other way round. The lactose intolerant person's body has reacquired the original human metabolism, and so it is actually those of us who still consume them with relish who are the ones with the real dietary problems, with our love of butter and cheese on our daily bread resulting in excessive weight gains.

THE CELTS

If I had to sum up one item of food that really says 'Celtic', it would have to be bacon or ham. The first Celtic society in Europe came from the Hallstatt region of Austria, where the famous salt mines are today. These people were in fact salt miners, and when archaeologists came across their remains in the labyrinth of tunnels in the Hallstatt mountains, they were well preserved due to the salt surrounding them. The Romans even commented on the fine quality of their salt pork and salt lamb, which were sold at the time in the markets as far south as Rome. So if you want to make yourself a quick and tasty authentic Celtic breakfast, make yourself a bacon sandwich with butter on brown bread and you are eating a bit of Celtic history!

On the whole, Celtic food was simple and unadulterated with lots of meat, fish, bread and butter and chunks of cheese. Their main vegetable crops were beans and peas, and the rest of their vegetables they still gathered from the surrounding countryside and seashore. Vegetables were primarily leaves and stems, as the root vegetables we know today only arrived in Britain at the time of the Roman Conquest.

I devised the recipes below from a variety of sources from the archaeological record. Until I wrote my other book, *Prehistoric Cooking*, no one had attempted to try and discover what recipes our prehistoric forbears might have used. There was a school of thought argu-

ing that, unless you found the actual residue of a particular meal in a pot, then you could not say categorically that our ancestors ate it. I, however, approached the subject in a different way. If we watch a TV documentary about an Amazonian tribe, we all assume that if there were tasty plants near them in the forest they would have known about them and eaten them. So I did not see why our ancestors should have been any different. I started to look at the pollen record around prehistoric settlements and, if the plants were tasty, then I put them in my recipes. I also looked at some lesser-known cooking techniques such as clay baking and water pit cooking. Residues of these were found by the archaeologists, but no one, other than myself over the last 16 years, had really experimented with them in any detail.

There are also some lesser-known quotes by classical historians about the Celtic diet that add to this picture. Interestingly, we all assume that if you are going back as far as the Celtic period, something as basic as bread might be a bit hard and chewy, but this was not the case, as a quotation from Pliny, the Roman historian, illustrates:

> When the corn of Gaul and Spain of the kinds we have stated is steeped to make beer the foam that forms on the surface in the process is for leaven, in consequence of which those races have a lighter kind of bread than others.

He is clearly talking about yeasted bread, which we tend to think was not eaten until much later. On the whole, the Celtic diet was varied, healthy and very tasty. One year I was doing a lot of cookery demonstrations and I found it impossible to weed my vegetable patch, as the weeds that grew around my vegetables were more valuable to me for cooking than the vegetables themselves! Here is a selection of recipes for you to try.

Lamb Stew
(For A Large Party Of 45 People)

I have made this stew many times for large public events and it always goes down very well. It can be adapted to suit vegetarian diets, too, by missing out the meat and frying a large quantity of chopped hazelnuts with the leeks in the butter.

1½ kg chopped or minced lamb
1 kg leeks — as an alternative to the wild onion Ramsons (*Allium ursinum*)
1 good bunch of sorrel (*Rumes Acetosella*)
1 bunch of chickweed (*Stellaria media*)
2 bunches of chives
3 kg peas
2 large sprigs of mint
4 tsp salt
2 kg Bulgar wheat (this is chopped, pre-cooked and dried wheat)

Method

1. Fry the lamb in a large pan until browned – there should be enough fat in the lamb without having to add any more.
2. Add the chopped sorrel, chives, leeks and chickweed and cook until tender.
3. Add the peas, mint, salt and enough water to cover it.
4. Simmer for approximately 30 minutes.
5. Add the Bulgar wheat and simmer until all the stock has been absorbed.

Serve preferably in wooden bowls and eat at once.

Lamb Boiled with Green Grass

This is the way people in prehistoric times cooked their meat in water pits. They covered the joint of meat, in this case a leg of lamb, in fresh green grass and tied it with string. Then they put it into a water pit and added hot stones to simmer for an hour or two until it was cooked. The grass not only protected the meat from the ash and stone grit in the trough, but also added flavour to the meat. Once cooked, the meat was taken out of its grass wrapping and crisped by the fire. This can be done in a modern kitchen by wrapping a leg of lamb in green grass and boiling it in a pot on the stove. When it is cooked, take it out of the grass and crisp it in the oven. You will never taste more delicious lamb than that is cooked in this way. The grass seems to bring out its real flavour.

Clay baked Trout with Ramsons

After gutting the trout, stuff it with chopped Ramson bulbs (or leeks), butter and a little salt. Tie tightly at least two layers of Ramson leaves or green leek leaves around the fish, and then cover in a flour and water paste. Tie on top of this a good layer of dried grasses and finally some silty clay (for instance, clay like that you might dig out of your garden) or foil. Cook the clay- or foil-covered fish in an open fire or in the oven for about an hour. Break the clay or remove the foil, and you will find that this fish is truly wonderful. The flour dough coating seals the Ramson or leek leaves in with the butter and the Ramson bulbs, and it tastes like garlic-buttered fish. Look out for the wild Ramsons in shady places and woodlands if you go for a walk in the spring; you will smell them long before you see them. This is a recipe well worth trying and would be a signature recipe for any top chef, if he made it!

BEACH BBQ IDEAS

Shellfish and Bacon Kebabs

Peel a willow stick and trim one end into a spike (or use a skewer). Skewer some oysters or scallops wrapped in sea beet leaves (or use spinach) with bacon, or any other combination – perhaps wild mushrooms, bacon and shellfish combinations. Roast them over a fire until cooked. For something really unusual and tasty you could gather seaweed to wrap the shellfish in to give extra flavour to the kebabs. No seaweed is poisonous in Britain, but it is important that you pick it from an unpolluted beach.

Ash-Cooked Shellfish

Make a herb butter with chervil and a little salt or celery seed. Arrange any shellfish you have into the hot ash at the edge of your beach fire. As the shells open, add a small piece of the herb butter and eat at once with bread. Once experienced, you will not have a beach fire again without these tasty treats!

Savoury Bean Fritters

These are made with the tinned Borlotti beans that you can find in any supermarket today; they are the nearest thing to the British field bean that the Celts used to grow. The skins are tough, though, so once drained, mash them with a fork before using. These two recipes are great high protein portable foods, savoury and sweet for those long winter walks and children love them.

125 g butter
1 bunch of sorrel (*Rumes Acetosella*)
125 g chopped hazelnuts
1 bunch of sea beet (*Beta vularis*) or Fat Hen (*Chenopodium album*) – spinach will do if you can't get these.
1 tbsp of grated horseradish
500 g processed beans (mashed with a fork)
1 egg

Salt to taste
Flour to mix
Method
1. Fry the sorrel in butter with the hazelnuts and sea beet, then add the grated horseradish and the beans.
2. Add the egg and salt and enough flour to make a stiff mixture.
3. Shape into rissoles and fry in more butter until brown.
These are good hot or cold.

Sweet Bean Cakes

These are a family favourite.
250 g butter
500 g whole-wheat flour
500 g processed beans (mashed with a fork)
500 g honey
125 g chopped hazelnuts
Method
1. Rub the butter into the flour and add the beans.
2. Stir in the honey and hazelnuts.
3. Cook spoonfuls of the mixture on a hot griddle until light brown on both sides.
This could be made at any time of the year because all the ingredients are easily stored. They are very nutritious and make a great snack.

Celtic sweet bean cakes. These are a real must to make for a healthy snack to take on a family walk

Wild Salad and Nettle Crisps

A wild salad is still available in the countryside of Britain if you go out there and look for it with a good plant book. The main ingredient of a spring wild salad would be any combination of the following:

Jack-by-the-hedge (*Alliaria petiolata*)
Dandelion (*Taraxacum officinale*)
Bedstraw (*Galium sp.*)
Shepherd's purse (*Capsella bursa-pastoris*)
Sheep's sorrel (*Rumes Acetosella*)
Hawthorn leaves (*Crataegus monogyna*) – in spring only, as they are too tough by summer
Beech leaves (*Fagus sylvatica*)
Chives (*Allium schoenoprasum*)

Then add some of these flowers if available to sprinkle on top with some salt.

Clover (*Trifolium sp.*)
Chives (*Allium schoenoprasum*)
Gorse (*Ulex Europaeus*)
Primrose (*Primila vulgaris*)
Violet (*Viola ordorata*)
Heather (*Calluna vulgaris*)
Elderflowers (*Sambucus nigra*)

For a really nice addition to the salad, add some crispy fried nettle leaves (*Urtica dioica*). These are surprisingly tasty. Prepare as follows:

Pick some young nettle leaves, wash and dry them in a cloth. Heat a pan with some butter or bacon fat and add the nettle leaves. Fry until crisp. When cold, crush and add a little salt and sprinkle on the wild salad as flavouring.

Rock Samphire (*Crithmum maritimum*)

This is my favourite wild vegetable. I eagerly wait for the spring when I can go down to the beach and collect it. Samphire grows on the rocks by the shore and is a succulent little plant with yellow umbellifer flowers. In sixteenth-century Britain there was quite an industry picking the Samphire and transporting it in barrels of brine to markets in London for sale there. It would have been a useful food source in the winter for prehistoric people too, who lived near the shorelines of Europe. It will keep fresh in strong salt brine for a year, and was soaked in vinegar for a day before use.

Fried Rock Samphire

The simplest and nicest way to eat it is to boil it in water until soft. Drain and fry it in butter until crisp. This is a wonderfully interesting and tasty food to serve to friends at a barbecue. It can also be served just boiled with melted butter.

Seaweed Pudding with Blackberry Juice

I am sure that in prehistoric times, every possible use would have been made of this particular food. Its sweetness and flavour would have been eagerly awaited during the winter, spring and early summer months. *Carragheen*, sometimes known as Irish Moss, can still be picked from the mid shore around our coasts. As I mentioned earlier, though, do make sure the beach you pick it from is not polluted.

1 kg blackberries
1 litre water
125 g dried *Carragheen* (Irish Moss)

Method

1. Bring the blackberries and water to the boil in a pot and simmer for 1 hour.
2. Strain and return fruit juice to the pot.
3. Add the seaweed (*Carragheen*) and simmer for another 30 minutes until dissolved.
4. Pour into a bowl to set.

When cold, this is a wonderful fruit jelly and can be served with cream.

BREAD CUPS

These recipes are for what the archaeologists call 'bread cups'. These carbonised bread cups have been found on Celtic sites in Britain and in Europe. They were made in prehistory by rolling out a simple flour and water dough into side plate-sized circles. These were then laid on top of hot, smooth, water-worn stones that had

Sea beet and curd cheese fritters. Make sure you pick the top leaves when you collect the Sea beet as the bottom leaves are usually a bit tough

Bread cups with fried apple and honey. All you need to make the bread cups are some round granite stones from the beach you can heat up in your oven. Make sure the stones are granite as slate will explode if you heat it. If you are not sure which is which ask someone from a natural history museum who will know been in the fire, so that the bread cooked itself from the heat of the stones and formed itself into a bowl shape when removed. If you can get hold of some round, volcanic beach pebbles, put them on a tray in the oven until they are very hot. Then place the dough over them carefully and cook for 25 minutes until they brown. (These can also be made by rolling the dough over some small metal pudding basins in the oven.) After you have taken the bread off the stones, put them (using an oven cloth) into a bowl of cold water and you will see how easy it was to get hot water in prehistoric times! Once you have cooked your bread cups, you can add a variety of fillings. These are wonderful to take on a picnic, but if you are going to try and cook them authentically over hot stones, make sure that the stones are igneous or volcanic or they will explode when put in the fire. If you are in doubt about the stones, please find out before you try this, as sedimentary stones put into any fire can be very dangerous.

Here are a few suggested fillings for your cooked bread cups. I made the smoked fish, leek and nut ones for a *Time Team* programme and they were very popular with Tony Robinson and the film crew!

Bread Cup Fillings

Plum and Honey Venison Bread Cups

2 venison steaks
100 g honey
500 g wild plums or small black plums
28 g butter
Method
1. Fry the plums in the butter, then add the finely chopped venison steaks. When cooked add the honey and cook gently for five more minutes so as not to burn the honey.
2. Fill the bread cups with this filling.
This is very good hot, but absolutely delicious cold for a picnic.

Bacon, Leek and Thyme Bread Cups

500 g leeks
250 g fatty bacon, chopped
28 g butter
1 tbsp fresh thyme leaves, chopped
Method
1. Fry the bacon until crispy and add the leeks and butter and finely chopped fresh thyme.
2. Simmer until the leeks are soft then fill the bread cups with this mixture.
These are best eaten hot, as the leeks do not taste so good when they are cold.

Smoked Fish, Leek and Nut Bread Cups (as seen on TV)

500 g leeks
125 g chopped hazelnuts
50 g butter
250 g smoked fish (any)
50 g double cream
Method
1. Fry the nuts in the butter and add the chopped leeks, cook until the leeks are tender.
2. Add the smoked fish and the cream and fill the bread cups with this mixture.
Three of the *Time Team* presenters were vegetarian, so I just gave them the same mixture omitting the fish. They liked it so much that one of them said he was going to try it as soon as he got home!

Sea Beet, Curd Cheese and Egg Bread Cups

500 g sea beet or spinach
200 g curd cheese (cottage cheese is good)
2 large eggs
Salt to taste
Method
1. Cook the sea beet or spinach until it is soft and then chop finely.
2. Mix the cheese with the eggs and salt and stir into the beet, then cook until the eggs are set and spoon into the bread cups.
This is very good hot or cold as a vegetarian pie to take on an expedition.

Here is a sweet version of the filled bread cups:

Hazelnut and Berry Bread Cups

300 g hazelnuts chopped

75 g butter

150 g honey

500 g mixed berries (any mixture e.g. blueberries, raspberries, blackberries and wild strawberries)

Method

1. Fry the chopped nuts with the butter and add the honey. Cook gently so as not to burn the honey and then add the berries.

2. Fill the cups with this mixture for a real treat.

PREHISTORIC SOLSTICE FEAST

Of course it would not be a Christian festival during the prehistoric period, it would have been a Winter Solstice festival. This was a very important festival for the Celts because it meant that the days were getting lighter again.

Breakfast on Feast Day

A bacon sandwich! For a feast day treat they might have indulged themselves with a slice of wholesome bread liberally spread with butter and eaten with lots of bacon crisped on stones by the fire.

Any Spit-Roasted Meat (apart from Chicken)

A large spit-roasted boar or deer would have been a favourite if the hunters had been successful. Chickens in the Celtic period, however, were very small bantam-like birds and not a particularly special meal.

Smoked Fish Stew

This is of course a store cupboard meal, as there would have always been one or two of their cows in milk at that time to provide the cream for this appetising dish. I have made this so many times in outdoor conditions and it is always delicious and so quick to make.

125 g bacon

2 leeks

500 g of any mixed smoked fish

1 litre of milk

300 ml cream

2 tbsp chives

1 tsp salt

Method

1. Fry the bacon until the fat comes away from it and add the chopped leeks. Cook until tender.

2. Add the fillets of fish and cover with the milk.

3. Slowly cook in a pot near the fire until the fish is cooked, which takes about 30 minutes.

4. Pour in the cream, along with the chopped chives and salt.

This is very good eaten with chunks of home-made bread for dipping.

Whole Salmon Baked in Clay

3 kg salmon

2 tbsp celery seed

1 tsp salt

A bunch of sorrel

A bunch of chives

Lots of long grass (green or dried)

String

Clay (silt clay i.e. the sort you would dig up in your garden or along a stream bank)

Method

1. Stuff the salmon with the herbs, salt it and sprinkle with celery seed.

2. Cover the fish in grass, either dried or fresh green grass if you have some in your garden.

3. Tie it tightly with string.

4. Smear a plank of wood with clay and put the fish on it, then cover it completely with the rest of the clay.

5. Put it next to an open fire or BBQ to dry the clay, and then slide it off the board and drop it into the fire. Build the fire or BBQ over it and keep it going for at least 1½ hours.

6. Break open the clay covering and remove the grass and enjoy. (This is the only way my son Dominic will eat salmon!)

If you do not want to use an open fire, then follow the instructions up to stage 3, cover it with foil and bake in an oven for the same amount of time. If you are eating the salmon cold then leave it in its casing of either clay or foil until it has cooled and it will be so deliciously juicy. I have never been able to do this successfully because whenever there is a group of people around me they always eat it all before it has a chance to go cold!

Fried Crab Apple and Honey Bread Cups

Honey was always saved for festivals in prehistory as it was mostly wild honey and not always easy to come by. This recipe makes good use of it though.

1 kg crab apples or cooking apples (cored and sliced)

75 g butter
200 g honey
200 g brown breadcrumbs
Ready-made bread cups
Method
1. Fry the apple slices in the butter until the apple starts to brown.
2. Drain and pour the remaining butter in the breadcrumbs with the honey and mix well.
3. Put a layer of the honey and breadcrumbs in the cups then a layer of the fried sour apples, and then top with more breadcrumbs.
4. Eat either when hot or cold with cream. They are very sweet, but with the sour centres they are incredibly moreish.

Bread baked in Honey

In one of the ancient Irish texts about the Feast of Bricriu, it says that 'He gathered food for a whole year, and he built a house at Dun Rudraige from which to serve it.'

Clay baked fish. You can cook this by wrapping it with grass just the same and covering it with foil instead of clay. You get the same taste and it is not so messy

There exists a list of the food that was pre-pared for this monumental feast, and the last part of the menu stated: '100 wheaten loaves baked in honey'. It seemed strange to me that this particular quotation did not describe 100 wheaten loaves with honey, or 100 wheaten honey loaves. It described the loaves as *baked* in honey. At an open-air cooking demonstra-tion, I decided to try this wheaten loaf baked in honey in a stone bank oven. This is an oven that is cut into an earthen bank and lined with large granite stones. A small hole is left at the back of the oven to allow the smoke to escape when a fire is lit inside. After a fire has been roaring for about an hour in the oven, the ashes are brushed out and a bowl containing the fresh fruit bread dough floating in honey was put into it. Any fruit-laden bread dough recipe can be used for this, but I found one with fresh wild plums that is very nice. I poured a litre of runny honey into a ceramic bowl and dropped the dough into this in one piece. I have to say that I was convinced the honey would burn when it was put into this very hot oven. The stone was placed to seal the oven and grass turf was put over the cracks to seal the heat in. After two hours, however, the oven door was opened and to my amazement the fruit bread was cooked to perfection. The honey had not burnt at all and had partly seeped into the bread dough, making a delightfully sticky prehistoric equivalent to a Rum Baba without the rum! Well worth trying at a winter bonfire party or in your oven at home for a Solstice feast.

Oat and Barley Bread

If you have any room left, follow your feast with lots of oat and barley bread and chunks of cheese.

750 g medium oatmeal
750 g barley flour (you can get this at a health food shop)
250 g butter
1 tsp salt
Milk to mix
Method
1. Mix together the oatmeal and the flour and add the salt.
2. Rub the butter in well.
3. Add enough milk to make a soft dough. The oatmeal absorbs a lot of liquid, so keep adding it in small amounts.
4. Shape into small flat cakes and cook on a griddle or a dry frying pan until firm and brown. This takes about 5 minutes on each side. This is a lovely savoury bread to eat with cheese and has a unique cheesy flavour all of its own.

Honey Drinks

The Celts always sweetened their stored beer or fruit wine with honey just before drinking it, so in a way, everything had a meady taste. At festival time they would have probably put more honey into the beer as a treat. So buy some real ale and add a few tablespoons of honey to it. Heat it in a pot from inside with a hot stone or a clean fire poker, and sprinkle some fresh herbs of your choice into it for a hot, festive honey drink.

THE ROMANS

The Romans were the first people to colonize Britain in the true sense of the word, stamping their architecture and culture on those that lived here before. After the initial resistance of the Celts to the invasion, the Romans put into action their method of taking over the minds and souls of the peoples they invaded. Firstly they gave them jobs in their country villas and cities and invited them to share some of the exotic foods they imported. Then they put on mass entertainments for the workers, including the circus, gladiator fights and chariot races. Large numbers of Celts were therefore slowly tempted into living this British version of the Roman way of life. The Roman settlements, however, did bring great changes to our countryside. They brought with them the concept of planting fodder crops i.e. crops primarily designed to be fed to animals to keep them healthy throughout the winter. Previously in the Celtic settlements, when the grazing and hay ran out, the animals not needed for breeding were slaughtered and the meat was preserved for the winter. This practice was incorporated into their Winter Solstice festival, when they acknowledged the darkest time of the winter and celebrated the return of the light.

As well as fodder crops, the Romans brought most of the plants we still grow in our vegetable patches today. If one reads Pliny's *The History,* it is just like a TV gardening book you might buy at Christmas. He details all you need to know about growing vegetables and even how to make pelleted seeds. I thought we had invented that in the 1970s, but no, Pliny describes how one should push a seed into a sheep or goat dropping and then plant it in the ground, ensuring that it has enough food surrounding it to supply the germinating plant.

Vegetables were the staple food of most Romans, and so it was incredibly important to them to improve their gardening techniques. Their favourite vegetable was the cabbage, of which they grew five distinct varieties. Root vegetables and onions were important too, as they could be preserved throughout the winter. While meat was enjoyed, it was outclassed by fish, egg and vegetable recipes.

The spice markets of southern Asia were the focal point of the Roman traders in their desire to collect more and more exotic spices for the tables of the Roman nobility. These spices became common and plentiful in Britain as the Roman occupation became established. Pepper, cinnamon, cumin, nutmeg, ginger and cloves were transported by ship from India, Sri Lanka, the Bay of Bengal, the Spice Islands and China. The flow and frequency of this trade at the time of the Roman Empire was not replicated again in Britain until the return of the Crusaders in the eleventh century.

In Roman gardens they grew 32 varieties of apples, 34 varieties of pears and 44 varieties of figs. This was incredible, as even our most pres-

Ramsons (prehistoric onions). You will know you have the right plants as you can smell the wild onions some time before you get to them on a hot day

tigious grocers could not contemplate stocking 34 varieties of pears, for instance. Peaches came from Persia, pomegranates from Tunisia, apricots from Armenia and cherries from the Near East. These fruits would have been imported for the Roman nobility that colonized Britain, but there would always have been leftovers for the servants too, I am sure. Those strange fruits and spices would have been a complete revelation to the local British workforce that maintained and ran their villas.

Apart from potatoes, tomatoes and sweet-corn they grew most of the vegetables we grow today. But that is where the similarity stops. The high-ranking Romans felt that they were too sophisticated and refined to just boil some carrots, say, and eat them with a sprinkling of salt. They had to change the look of their food to make a vegetable look like a fish and vice versa. They would instruct their servants go to considerable lengths to hide the

natural forms of their foodstuffs. They would not even sprinkle their food with salt; as that was far too simplistic for their palates, they had to make a fermented fish sauce called *Garum* or *Liquium* with which to season their food. Thanks to the wealth of literature left by the Romans, it is reasonably easy to find recipes for the Roman people.

The average person in a Roman British town would live in an apartment just as most Italians do today, and these apartments would not have had kitchens. So people would eat a light breakfast of bread and fruit and at midday they would eat cold meat or fish with bread. In the evening, however, they would go and get a takeaway from the wealth of street-fronted establishments in their towns. In Pompeii there is a good example at a place called Arsellina's tavern, where this street-fronted bar had sunken pots in the counter to serve steaming hot food to the passing trade. The type of food served in these pots could be something like lentil stew or lamb in plum sauce or pork and leek sausages – all of which are recipes for you to try in this chapter. The lentil stew, which incorporates cumin powder and fresh dill, does sound a little odd, but I have tried it many times and it is really delicious. Most of us think our takeaway city culture in Britain is a very modern phenomenon, but it was actually going on 2,000 years ago!

A Roman called Marcus Apicius wrote a cookery book that shows in detail what the Roman nobility ate. He was a decadent gourmet during the first century AD. He was said to actually teach Haute Cuisine, and his love of fine foods was actually his downfall in the end, for his lavish dining extravaganzas had made him bankrupt and he was said to have taken his own life with poison during one last fantastic meal, rather than eat like the poor people.

A poet of the time, Martial, wrote this poem about Apicius's demise:

> After you'd spent 60 million on your stomach,
>   Apicius,
> 10 million still remained,
> An embarrassment, you said fit only to satisfy
>   mere hunger and thirst:
> So your last and most expensive meal was
>   poison …
> Apicius, you never were more than a glutton
>   than at the end.

I think that poor Apicius would have been delighted to know that his own recipes were still being made over 2,000 years later. Another typical Apicius tale is this one, related by a historian called Athenaeus:

> Apicius of extraordinary wealth … passed his time for the most part eating very costly prawns of the region of Campania … He happened to hear that prawns also grew enormous size off the Libyan coast [all of Africa

was called Libya at the time]. Accordingly he set sail that very day. After suffering from storms during the voyage across the open sea he drew near to the land.

Apparently when he got there, he found the prawns were no bigger than the ones he ate in Italy, so he had the boat turned around and went straight home, such was his dedication to his palate.

Just as a point of interest on the Roman food front, there has been some new research from the University of Vienna on the diet of Roman gladiators. They tested the bones of gladiators from a gladiator graveyard in Ephesus in modern day Turkey, and were shocked to discover that the diet of those prime fighting men was mainly made up of vegetables and barley – just carbohydrates, with very little, if any, meat proteins. The reason for this was found in historical accounts, that the gladiators had to have a good layer of fat on them in order to keep fighting once wounded. A thin gladiator would be dispatched too quickly, as glancing blows of the sword would be able to cut into their internal organs. The fat layer apparently let the fighters carry on long after they were wounded. This diet would have given the gladiators a serious calcium deficiency, but historical accounts say that they were made to drink bone ash to keep their bones strong. Somehow one imagines the Hollywood versions of the gladiators as slim muscular men, rather than ones carrying a good layer of fat to protect them in battle!

ROMAN INGREDIENTS FOR COOKING

The famous Roman fish sauce, *Garum* or *Liquamen*, was made in factories around the Empire and transported to all corners of it in amphora to season savoury food. It was made by putting the entrails of oily fish into great vats with salt and fermenting it for six months in the hot sun. This sauce was used in almost every Roman recipe. The simplest equivalent is *Nam Pla*, the Thai fish sauce that is readily available in Britain today.

In a lot of the original recipes they use rue, fleabane and other mildly toxic herbs to add bitterness to dishes. The most exact equivalent is angostura bitters, as it will do the same job without running the risk of poisoning yourself!

Boiled wine is used in a lot of recipes too, so if you are planning on doing a lot of Roman cooking it would be best to make a batch. Just boil either red or white wine until it is reduced by half, and then bottle it for future use.

COLD FOOD

This food can be prepared well in advance to make a wonderful Roman feast for your friends to enjoy. All the Roman desserts were cold and these can be enjoyed at any Roman banquet. In the Roman period, homemade desserts were really rare, and so a huge bowl of succulent fruit (especially peaches, fresh figs and grapes) is actually more authentic, and is a definite must on any buffet table.

Boiled Egg and Anchovy

This is a very simple recipe, but the Romans did tend to play with their food, making it look like it was something else. They were known to make hare or kid or sometimes chicken livers into the shape of a fish. They made vegetables look like meat in the same way. For a TV pro-gramme, I made this recipe into a fish shape, and this would look good on a buffet table.

8 hard-boiled eggs
1 tin anchovies
50 g raisins
50 g pine nuts
1 tbsp vinegar
1 tbsp oil
(Flaked almonds and one pea if you are going to make a fish shape)
Method
1. Chop the eggs and the anchovies and mix in the raisins and pine nuts, vinegar and oil until it is like dough.
2. Lay some radicchio lettuce leaves on a platter and put the egg dough onto it. Shape it to look like a large fish.
3. Layer the flaked almonds along the body of the fish to replicate scales and press a green pea on it in place of its eye.

Bread Salad

This is a great accompaniment for any cold Roman savoury dish, or could be served on a buffet in slices.
1 loaf of good quality white bread
100 ml mild vinegar
100 ml water
250 g grated cheese, such as Cheshire or Caerphilly
1 tbsp honey
3 cloves garlic
A pinch of pepper
A small sprig of mint
A large bunch fresh coriander
75 g chopped spring onions
30 ml olive oil
50 ml white wine vinegar
3 tbsp water
Salt to taste
Method
1. Remove the crust off the top of the loaf and hollow it out.
2. Soak the bread you have taken out with vin-egar and water and set it aside.
3. Cover the bottom of the loaf with half the grated cheese.
4. Chop the herbs and mix with the other ingredients.
5. Add this to the bowl of soaked breadcrumbs and mix well together.

A Roman bread salad. I was not sure how this recipe would turn out, but found it really delicious and have added it to my summer picnic menu

6. Fill the loaf with the ingredients and top with the rest of the cheese.

7. Chill well before serving in slices.

Scallop Rissoles (made to look like Parsnips)

24 scallops

¼ tsp pepper

1 tsp fish sauce

1 egg beaten

50 g flour

Salt and pepper to taste

Sprigs of rosemary leaves for decoration (if you are going to shape into parsnips)

Method

1. Quickly fry the scallops in some oil and set to one side.

2. Chop the cooked scallops finely and put in a bowl.

3. Add the pepper and fish sauce and the beaten egg.

4. Mix well and shape into cones the shape of a parsnip, or just rissoles if you are not shaping it.

5. Roll in seasoning flour and fry gently in olive oil until browned on all sides, keeping the shape intact. Stuff some sprigs of rosemary leaves in the end to replicate the parsnip tops and serve as a starter or on a cold buffet.

Sweet Date Chicken Salad

500 g cooked chicken meat cut into cubes

¼ tsp pepper

2 tbsp chopped parsley

200 g chopped dates

1 bunch chopped spring onions

150 ml wine

1 tbsp white wine vinegar

Method

1. Put the dates, pepper, wine and wine vinegar in a pan.

2. Simmer gently until the dates have absorbed the liquid.

3. Stir in the onions, parsley and the cooked chicken.

4. Put on a serving dish and serve cold.

Onion Relish for Ham

4 large onions

A handful of fresh thyme

A handful of fresh oregano

125 g chopped dates

2 tbsp honey

2 tbsp vinegar

75 ml boiled wine

1 tbsp olive oil

2 tbsp onion stock

Method

1. Boil the onions in lots of water and drain and save a little stock.

2. Chop the cooked onions finely when cold.

3. Add all the other ingredients and chill for 24 hours before use.

4. Serve with ham or cold fish.

HOT FOOD

The origins of the Italian lasagne can clearly be seen in this recipe from Apicius's book.

The Original Lasagne

Meat or fish sauce

500 g cooked chicken or 500 g cooked filleted fish or 500 g cooked pork

3 eggs

¼ tsp pepper

1 tsp celery seeds

300 ml stock (chicken, fish or pork)

150 ml sweet wine

150 ml dry white wine

3 tbsp olive oil

Flour to thicken the sauce

125 g pine nuts

Dough

500 g flour

250 ml olive oil

1 tbsp salt or fish sauce

Water to mix

Method

1. Make a soft dough with the flour, oil and water.

2. Roll out into four circles the size of the oven-proof dish it is to be cooked in and set aside.

3. Mix the meat or fish with the other ingredients (apart from the eggs) in a pan and bring to the boil.

4. Simmer for 20 minutes, adding more stock if needed to keep it liquid.

5. Whisk in the eggs to thicken the sauce.

6. Lay one of the dough circles in the base of the dish and ladle some of the meat or fish sauce over it.

7. Repeat this process until you finish with the dough on the top.

8. Make some holes in the top crust and brush with beaten egg and sprinkle with pepper.

9. Bake slowly in an oven for 1 hour until all the dough layers are cooked between the meats.

10. Leave to stand for 30 minutes after taking out of the oven and cutting into squares.

Roman Army Lentil Stew

100 g green lentils

1 medium onion

125 ml red wine

1 tsp cumin seeds

1 tsp dried dill or a bunch of fresh dill

A sprig of thyme

A sprig of oregano

A handful of fresh parsley

1 tbsp olive oil

Black pepper and sea salt to taste

Roman Army lentil stew. This stew really looks disgusting being a sludgy green colour but it tastes really delicious. In Roman times there was said to be a fashion one year to make ugly looking food to play a joke on your guests to see if they were polite enough to try it. This recipe would suit this really well

Method

1. Slice the onion thinly and fry gently in olive oil until soft and just beginning to turn golden brown.

2. Add 600 ml of water, the red wine and the lentils.

3. Using a pestle and mortar grind the cumin and aniseed together and add this to the mixture along with the dill.

4. Bring the mixture to the boil and simmer for 45 minutes, or until the lentils have cooked through. Make sure that all the liquid has boiled away so that the lentils are almost dry.

5. Stir in the finely-chopped thyme and oregano. Mash lightly with a fork and tip into a bowl. Garnish with chopped parsley or thyme and serve.

Pork and Leek Sausages

We all think of pork and leek sausages as a modern invention, at least I did until I saw Apicius's recipe. It is spicier and has ground almonds in it, but it is still a pork and leek sausage. Interestingly, Apicius suggested these sausages were boiled in pork stock, like frankfurters, and once cooked, they were browned under a grill.

450 g minced pork

225 g fine breadcrumbs

2 leeks, finely chopped

125 g cooked bacon, chopped

50 g ground almonds

1 tsp pepper

2 tsp celery seeds

1 egg beaten

A saucepan of pork stock
Sausage casings
Method
1. In a bowl mix the pork, breadcrumbs, leeks, bacon and almonds well.
2. Add the celery seed and pepper and bind with an egg.
3. Put into casings or shape into sausage shapes.
4. If using casings, boil in stock for 30 minutes then brown in the oven.
5. If not using casings, roast on a tray in a hot oven for 30 minutes.
Serve hot or cold.

Mushrooms in Honey

25 g dried porcini mushrooms
2 tbsp red wine vinegar
1 tbsp clear honey
Salt to taste
Method
1. Put mushrooms in a bowl, cover with boiling water and allow them to soak for 1 hour.
2. Pour the mushrooms and liquor into a pan, add the honey and vinegar and bring to the boil.
3. Cover and simmer for half an hour.
Season with salt and serve. This mushroom mixture goes particularly well with game.

Spiced Squash
(to look like a crab in seaweed)

1 medium-sized squash
½ tsp pepper
1 tsp ground cumin
1 tsp fresh ginger
2 drops of angostura bitters
1 tbsp wine vinegar
300 ml boiled red wine
300 ml stock
1 small squash to cut into crab claws to decorate the dish (parboil it before you cut it so it is not too brittle to shape)
2 raisins for the crab's eyes
1 small green cabbage like a Savoy

Method
1. Cut the squash flesh into chunks and boil until cooked.
2. Strain, keeping the stock, squeeze out the liquid and put it in a fresh pan.
3. Add to the pan all the other ingredients and simmer for 30 minutes or until all the liquid is absorbed.
4. Serve at once or, if you are going to shape it, follow the instructions below:
Put on a large serving dish and shape it into the body of a crab using the parboiled squash crab claws. You just have to make it into an oval dome with the claws coming out of it. Use the raisins for the eyes and put it on a platter of finely shredded boiled cabbage. Eat cold with cold meat or with fish and bread.

Spring Greens with Cumin

500 g spring greens
1 tsp cumin seeds
2 tbsp olive oil
300 ml stock
150 ml wine
1 tbsp fish sauce
Method
1. Shred the spring greens finely, including the stalks.
2. Heat the oil in a pan and add the cumin seeds until they start to crackle.
3. Add the shredded spring greens to the pan and stir well and cook for a further 5 minutes.
4. Pour in the stock and wine and simmer until cooked and until the liquid has evaporated.

Here are three different plum sauces for venison, lamb and duck. They are all very different and well worth trying:

Plum Sauce for Venison

2 kg roasted venison joint
A handful of chopped Lovage or celery leaves
2 tbsp parsley, finely chopped
500 g fresh plums, chopped

1 tbsp honey

150 ml red wine

1 tbsp vinegar

1 tbsp fish sauce

2 tbsp olive oil

250 ml stock

Method

1. Chop and stone the plums and cut into small chunks.

2. Put all the ingredients in a pan and stir slowly over the heat until the plums are soft.

3. Reduce the heat, cover and cook slowly for 1 hour.

4. Pour into a sauce boat and serve with roast venison.

Plum Sauce for Roast Lamb

2 kg roasted lamb

½ tsp ground ginger

½ tsp pepper

2 tbsp olive oil

½ tsp dried savoury

1 tsp fresh rosemary, finely chopped

225 g fresh plums, stoned and finely chopped

1 large onion, finely chopped

150 ml red wine

150 ml stock

2 tbsp wine vinegar

Method

1. Roast the lamb in the usual way.

2. Prepare the sauce by frying the onion in the oil and stir in the herbs. When the onion is soft, add the other ingredients (apart from the vinegar).

3. Simmer gently for 1 hour.

4. When the roast is cooked, put it on a platter and pour the hot sauce over it. Drizzle the vinegar over the sauce and serve.

Plum Sauce for Duck with a Pastry Crust

1 large duck

A pinch of peppercorns

250 g shallots

A large bunch of Lovage (or young celery leaves)

½ tsp cumin

½ tsp celery seeds

70 g stoned plums

50 ml red wine vinegar

50 ml fish sauce

50 ml grape juice

30 ml olive oil for sauce

200 g flour

Olive oil for pastry

Method

1. Make pastry with the flour and enough olive oil to bind the flour together. If too dry, add a few drops of water.

2. Season this with salt and pepper and cover the duck in a layer of pastry.

3. Place in a roasting tin and roast for 2 hours in a moderate oven.

4. Meanwhile, place all the herbs in a mortar and grind with a pestle.

5. Add this to a pan with the plums, vinegar, fish sauce, grape juice and 30 ml of olive oil.

6. Cook until the plums are tender.

7. Strain the sauce and pour over slices of duck and pastry.

Date and Herb Sauce for Poached Tuna

3 tuna fish steaks

¼ tsp pepper

½ tsp celery seeds

¼ tsp thyme

1 onion, finely chopped

125 g dates, chopped

1 tbsp honey

1 tbsp vinegar

1 tbsp fish sauce

1 tbsp olive oil

150 ml water

Method

1. Poach the tuna fish lightly in the usual way.

2. Sauté the onion in the oil until tender.

3. Add the herbs and cook for another minute.

4. Mix in the other ingredients and stir well.

5. Add the water and simmer until the water has been absorbed.

6. Spread this mix over the tuna steaks and serve immediately.

Stuffed Herrings or Stuffed Trout

2 cleaned fish with the heads and tails left on
¼ tsp pepper
½ tsp cumin seeds
1 tbsp fresh mint, chopped
200 g walnuts, chopped
1 tbsp honey
2 tbsp olive oil
4 tbsp boiled wine
2 tsp fish sauce

Method

1. Clean the fish, leaving the head and tail on.
2. Mix together the cumin, pepper, mint and walnuts and honey.
3. Stuff the fish with this mixture and put it in an ovenproof dish with a lid on. Bake for 35 minutes until the fish is cooked.
4. Mix together in a dish the olive oil, wine and fish sauce and heat through in a pan.
5. Put the fish on a serving dish and pour over the olive oil, boiled wine and fish sauce dressing and serve.

Nutty Egg Tart

1 tsp nutmeg
125 g chopped roasted hazelnuts
200 g honey
1 tbsp finely chopped fresh rosemary
4 tbsp sweet wine or sweet sherry
150 ml milk
2 eggs
Pastry to line a pie dish made with 225 g spelt flour and 100 g lard and water

Method

1. Mix the chopped roasted hazelnuts with half the honey, rosemary and the sweet wine.
2. Spread this over a pre-baked pastry case.
3. Beat the eggs in the milk with the rest of the honey and pour over the nut mixture.
4. Sprinkle with nutmeg and bake in a moderate oven for 35 minutes or until firm and golden to touch.
5. Take out of the oven and sprinkle with more roasted chopped hazelnuts (these should sink slightly into the custard mixture).
6. Leave until cold before cutting. Serve on a platter decorated with rosemary leaves.

Honey omelette

The Romans called this an egg sponge, but it is clearly an omelette.

4 eggs
300 ml milk
125 g runny honey
3 tbsp olive oil
Cinnamon to taste

Method

1. Beat the eggs in the milk.
2. Heat the oil in a pan and then pour in the egg mixture.
3. Reduce the heat and cook until it is set.
4. Put onto a platter and pour the honey over the omelette when it is still hot.
5. Sprinkle with cinnamon and serve hot.

Sweet Toast

This is the Roman equivalent of French toast but without the egg. It is very simple, but very nice too!

Half a loaf of sliced bread with the crusts cut off
300 ml of milk or enough to moisten the bread
3 tbsp olive oil
4 tbsp honey

Method

1. Soak the bread in the milk and drain excess off.
2. Heat the oil in the pan and, when hot, cook the bread in it until it is a golden colour.
3. Put onto a platter and drizzle with honey.
4. Eat with slices of fresh fruit.

A Dish of Spiced Pears

500 g hard pears
20 g honey
1 tbsp ground cumin

300 ml sweet wine

1 tsp olive oil

2 egg yolks

Method

1. Halve the pears and peel and core them.

2. Cover in water and poach until soft. Drain, keeping some of the liquid.

3. Into a pan, put 200 ml of the pear liquid, wine, cinnamon, egg yolks and oil and heat gently until thickened.

4. Add pears to the pan and heat through. Serve at once.

A Dish of Spiced Peaches

500 g unripe peaches

1 tbsp cumin

1 tsp olive oil

1 tbsp honey

Method

1. Stone and cut the flesh into cubes and cover with water.

2. Simmer until tender.

3. Drain and sprinkle with oil, honey and cumin.

4. Serve cold and add more honey if it is not sweet enough.

Barley Drink

450 g pearl barley

1 litre sweet white wine

200 g honey

Water – enough to cover barley when cooking

Method

1. Boil barley in water for 1 hour until cooked.

2. Drain, keeping liquid.

3. Mix in the wine with the barley water and sweeten to taste with honey.

4. Chill well before serving.

THE FIRST CHRISTMAS FEASTS

For the first three centuries after the Christian religion began, it was outlawed by the Roman Empire as we all know from our school text books. But what is little known is that the Romans were the first to celebrate the nativity on 25 December. The Emperor Constantine I became a Christian himself in AD 312 and from then on it became the official religion of the Roman Empire. Prior to this, the Romans had celebrated the Winter Solstice on 25 December. The earliest written record of the nativity being celebrated on this date was on an illuminated manuscript in Rome dated AD 354.

So the first lavish Christian nativity feasts would have been Roman. Apicius lived in the first century AD, but his cookbook was edited and republished in the fourth century AD, about the time of the first Christmas feasts. This is why Apicius's recipes were very likely to have been used during those original Christmas dinners.

So if you want to have a really original – in all senses of the word – Christmas dinner, why not try a Roman one!

Squash Alexandrine

1 medium-sized squash

½ tsp pepper

½ tsp cumin seeds

½ tsp coriander seeds

¼ cup chopped fennel bulb

2 tbsp chopped mint

2 tbsp cider vinegar

2 tbsp runny honey

150 ml boiled red wine

75 ml squash stock

2 tbsp olive oil

50 g chopped dates

50 g finely chopped walnuts

Method

1. Chop the squash flesh into cubes and boil until cooked.

2. Drain, saving the stock, and press out as much liquid as you can.

3. Sprinkle the cooked squash with salt and put in a pan.

4. Put the cumin, coriander, fennel, mint, nuts, dates, vinegar and honey in a blender or mortar and work until it is a paste.

5. Add this to the pan with the wine stock and olive oil and bring slowly to the boil. Simmer for 5 minutes.

6. Serve on a platter sprinkled with pepper and eat with chunks of bread.

Parsnips with Honey Sauce

6 large cooked parsnips
1 tbsp celery seeds
1 tsp finely chopped rosemary
2 tbsp runny honey
150 ml white wine
150 ml parsnip stock
1 tbsp olive oil
¼ tsp pepper
Flour to thicken

Method

1. Boil the sliced parsnips until tender and save the stock.

2. Mix celery seeds, rosemary, honey and pepper together in a pan with a little flour.

3. Add the other ingredients and bring to the boil, stirring until the sauce has thickened.

4. Pour over the parsnips and put in the oven to heat through for 10 minutes. Serve.

Nutty Scrambled Eggs

6 eggs
125 g pine nuts
125 g chopped hazelnuts
1 tbsp honey

Baked ham. The figs and ham are cooked together and their flavours work well

¼ tsp pepper

1 tsp anchovy sauce (this is sold in most supermarkets)

300 ml milk

1 tbsp olive oil

Anchovy fillets to decorate the dish

Method

1. Toast the pine nuts and hazelnuts in the oil in
a frying pan.

2. Beat the eggs with the milk and add the
anchovy sauce, honey and pepper.

3. Add the egg mixture to the pan with the
nuts, stirring constantly until the scrambled
eggs are cooked.

4. Serve onto a platter and decorate with more
pine nuts and anchovy fillets.

Cold Ham

2 kg ham

500 g dried figs

200 g runny honey

500 g spelt flour

150 ml olive oil

3 bay leaves

Method

1. Put the ham in water and bring to the boil.
Boil for 30 minutes.

2. Discard the water and cover again with fresh
water. Add the whole dried figs and the bay leaves.

3. Bring to the boil and simmer for 1 hour.

4. Drain, saving the figs, and when cold, take off
the skin of the ham.

5. Score the top into diamonds and drizzle the
honey into the cracks.

6. Make a dough with the flour oil and water
to mix.

7. Roll it out and cover the ham with it.

8. Bake for 30 minutes in a hot oven.

9. Serve in slices with the crust on when cold.

Apricot Relish for Ham

450 g whole fresh apricots (under ripe are best)

1 tsp cinnamon

1 tsp dried mint

3 tbsp honey

150 ml sweet muscatel wine

150 ml white wine

2 tbsp vinegar

2 tbsp olive oil

Pepper to taste

Method

1. Wash the apricots, stone them and put them
in a pan in halves.

2. Mix cinnamon, mint, honey, vinegar and oil
in a bowl.

3. Mix this with the wines and pour over the
apricots.

4. Simmer gently for 1 hour, adding a little
more wine if it becomes too dry.

5. When cold arrange the whole apricots in a
dish surrounded by the sauce.

Walnut and Fig Cakes

I made these for a TV programme and the
camera crew ate them all as soon as we had
finished filming, even though they all said they
didn't usually eat very sweet food!

Dough

450 g spelt flour

200 ml olive oil

Water to mix

Filling

200 g walnuts

200 g dried figs

75 g honey

125 g olive oil

75 g runny honey to serve with

Method

1. Mix the dough ingredients until pliable and
leave to chill for 1 hour.

2. Chop the dates and walnuts finely and mix in
the honey to make a paste.

3. Roll out the dough and cut into small rounds
(use a wine glass as a cutter).

4. Place a teaspoon of the filling in the centre of
each dough circle.

5. Moisten the edges and add another circle on
top so you have little flying saucer shapes.

Fig and walnut cakes. I first made these for a TV programme on Roman cooking and the camera crew ate them as soon as I made them!

Spiced wine Apicius. This is an easy and very interesting punch to make for a party

6. Put the oil in a frying pan and when hot, fry the pastries on both sides until golden brown.

7. Put onto a serving platter and drizzle with the rest of the honey. Serve hot or cold.

Dates Alexandrine

The cooking of these dates really changes the taste of them, as it caramelises the skin and is really delicious.

450 g whole dates
200 g whole blanched almonds
25 g cinnamon
125 g melted butter
200 g honey
Edible gold leaf to make them really special!
Method
1. Brush the almonds with butter and roll immediately in cinnamon.
2. Stuff one almond into the cavity of the date after the stone is removed.
3. Brush the date with warm honey.
4. Bake in a moderate oven for 5–10 minutes until the skin of the dates starts bubbling.

5. If you wish, you can place a strip of edible gold leaf on the dates for a festive look.
6. Lay them on a platter and serve with quarters of fresh figs or green grapes.

Spiced Wine Apicius

300 ml white wine
500 g honey
1 tsp pepper
½ tsp saffron
1 tsp cinnamon
4 dates, finely chopped
1 bay leaf
3½ quarts white wine
Method
1. Mix the 300 ml of wine with the honey in a pan and gently heat, stirring continuously.
2. Add the dates, pepper and saffron strands in a muslin bag with the bay leaf and the powdered cinnamon.
3. Add the rest of the wine and heat gently. Simmer for 1 hour over a very low heat.
4. Take the spice bag out and serve either warm with a starter or hot with a dessert.

THE ANGLO SAXONS

The Saxon invasion of Britain after the Romans abandoned it eventually forced the remaining Celts to move ever westward until they only survived on the Atlantic margins in Cornwall, Wales and Ireland. Those Romanised Britons who wished to stay in the Roman towns had to pledge new allegiances to the coarse Saxon warrior chieftains. It was at first very much a case of the Saxons being squatters occupying the areas where the Romans had lived. The Roman towns, with their defensive walls, were the first obvious places to inhabit. Once the Saxon warriors had subjugated the remaining Britons, waves of colonists arrived to settle in the rich British countryside. The abandoned Roman country estates were the natural places for those Saxon settlers to move to. Isolated though they were, they still had the remains of the Roman field systems and were usually well placed in the countryside, with good watercourses nearby. The settlers thrived with those rich soils that had been cultivated for over 400 years by the Romans. However, the Roman road systems that linked those isolated estates soon fell into disrepair, and the settlements became more isolated and rural and enjoyed less contact with the old Roman towns.

Those isolated Saxon farmsteads eventually gave way to communal settlements, and the English village was born. Villages today that have their names ending in 'ham' trace their origins to these first communal settlements, as 'ham' is the Saxon word for enclosure. Once the villages started to grow, they needed more land to cultivate and they started to clear the surrounding forests. So hamlets today ending in –den, –ley and –hurst are derived from the Saxon prefixes for newly cleared land. After Christianisation, churches were built in these villages and it was only then that the divide between the foods of the clergy and the foods of the farmers became so evident.

The ploughman in the field would be brought dark rye bread and skimmed milk cheese for his midday food, swilled down with watery ale. At the end of his day, he would return to his homestead when it was too dark to plough anymore and have the same bread and ale, possibly with a bowl of hot bean stew. On special occasions, they might have some fish or salt meat as a treat, but fresh meat was a luxury tasted only by the most prosperous farmers. This monotonous diet was only broken by the annual invitations to their feudal lord's great hall, when they would see how the other half lived, as it were. Those feasts would have been lavish affairs compared with the villagers' normal diet. Whole deer and wild boar would be spit roasted and the food would have been washed down with not just ale, but also with wine and sweet mead to the telling of stories and entertainments of all kinds.

Large monasteries were soon built in the countryside and as the church became more powerful, the abbot took the place of the feudal lord in many places. The difference between the lifestyle of the abbot and his monks and their Christian flocks soon became immense. Compare a simple pease pottage and black bread to the food required for by an abbot embarking on a few days' journey. The following passage comes from an ancient text:

> Wheat bread and a measure of honey and fish, butter, milk, lard, and cheese and eggs and toast and whipped cream and beef, pork and mutton, vegetables, peppered dishes and good beer, wine and mulled mead and every good thing and a napkin.

So the food of the Saxon villager consisted primarily of what they could make themselves, plus those yearned-for feasting days when they were invited to the Great Hall. In the towns, however, there were trade links with Europe, and trade for the wealthy wool merchants in towns like London was immense. Bede said of London at the time, 'an emporium of many peoples coming from land and sea.'

So when we look at the food of the Saxon period, it was poles apart depending on your status and whether you were a town or a country dweller. There are not really any recipes left from this period, or from the Viking period, just lists of ingredients found from the pollen record, or as residues in pots. They indicate that their diet was in some way similar to the Celtic diet: simple roasted or boiled meats and bread and cheese, broken up with ale and mead on special occasions.

THE NORMANS

The Norman invasion is remembered by every child in Britain because of the Battle of Hastings in 1066, when Harold was shot in the eye with an arrow. It was, however, just another Viking invasion under another name. The Normans or North Men were a group of Scandinavian raiders under the leadership of Rollo in AD 911, who sailed up the River Seine and forced the French king to cede some French territory on the north French coast. And so they settled in what we call Normandy today. It became an independent kingdom, with little interference from the French king over time. Even so, the Vikings who settled there very quickly adopted the religion, language and customs of the surrounding French population so that, by the time they did invade Britain, to all intents and purposes they were French Normans.

It was the Norman knights' trips to the Crusades and North Africa that really brought another dimension to the diet of this new British nobility. There are still today intact Norman castles at the very tip of Italy in Basilicata – once Norman territory – that are an extraordinary sight, looking so out of place in that vast landscape of dormant volcanoes.

When these knights returned, they had acquired a Middle Eastern palate full of spices and rich almond sauces. The Crusaders occupied the Holy Land from 1099–1187 and so, by the thirteenth century, the legacy of this association with Jerusalem had completely incorporated itself into the diet of the British nobility. The Crusaders ate sugar for the first time, which they called 'honey-cane', and they ate almonds, rice, dates, citrus fruits, pomegranates and rose water on a daily basis. Those spicy smells that came out of the Norman kitchens had not been smelt in Britain since the Roman occupation over 600 years earlier. Before the Crusades, the average staple food in Britain was pottage made of wheat for the rich, and barley, rye and oats for the poorer classes.

Most European cookery books from the thirteenth century show that this Saracen Arabic influence was widespread. The Norman territory in Sicily shared much of this Arabic Greek and Latin culture too. Crops such as sugar, rice, citrus, pomegranate and saffron were grown in the Arab occupied west, and saffron was eventually grown in England, hence the village name of Saffron Walden in Essex.

Until 1934, people thought that it was just the new food ingredients that influenced north western cuisine, but the discovery of some ancient manuscripts made academics realize that it was Arabic cooking methods, too, that were imported into Britain with them. In 1934 an Iraqi scholar called Dr Chelebi discovered some ancient manuscripts that were dated to the thirteenth century. It was in fact a cookbook written by Muhammad ibn al Hassan and was translated that year into English by a

Professor Arberry. The book (now known as *The Baghdad Cook Book*) was divided into ten chapters of dishes titled Sour, Milk (mainly yoghurt dishes), Plain, Fried, Dry, Simple, Sweet, Meat, Fish and Sauces, Pickles and Salads. The 160 recipes in this book showed historians that the Crusaders had brought back Arabic recipes to Britain. These had been incorporated into British food so widely that the spicy flavours were no longer regarded as foreign at all. In the book, it instructs the cook that meat should be cut up and browned in fat before being added to a stew with spices and vegetables. Before this time, meat was generally boiled in one piece with whole vegetables, not seared first. It is such an integral part of how we cook our meat today that it is amazing to think that it was actually a Saracen method of preparing stew.

Colouring food was also an Arab invention using saffron and other herbs to colour the drab, grey looking sauces and make them take on a new vibrancy. Red food colouring was made from Indian sandalwood, which came west in the spice ships with pepper and other spices. It was found that a cheaper version of this red food dye could be made with crushed wild rose hips, readily available in the English countryside. The recipes in this section are taken from early Medieval French sources too, as the new French noblemen would undoubtedly have brought their own cuisine with them to Britain.

These first seven recipes are taken from *The Baghdad Cook Book,* and show how much the Crusaders' travels into the Middle East influenced British and also French cuisine.

Lamb Stew with Mint and Spices

1½ kg lamb meat cut from the bone
Oil for frying
1 tsp salt
2 large onions
2 leeks
1 tsp ground coriander
1 tsp cumin

1 tsp cinnamon
300 ml yoghurt or sour milk
1 lemon
Bunch of fresh mint
Method
1. Put the meat in a pan and fry in oil until brown, then add the salt and cover with water. Boil, removing the scum as it forms. Reduce the heat and simmer for 30 minutes.
2. When the meat is nearly cooked, add the chopped onions and leeks to the pot.
3. Add the spices and keep cooking on a low heat until all the liquid evaporates.
4. Add the lemon, sliced thinly, and the yoghurt and the roughly chopped mint, and simmer for another 10 minutes. Serve with bread.

Lamb Stew with Mint and Apples

1 kg fatty lamb meat (breast of lamb is good)
2 chicken thigh joints
2 onions, chopped
1 tsp salt
1 tsp ground coriander
1 tsp cinnamon
½ tsp ginger
1 large bunch fresh mint
½ tsp pepper
450 g cooking apples
50 g blanched almonds (soaked in boiling water for 1 hour)
Method
1. Put the chopped lamb in a pan and brown with oil before adding the coriander and salt and cover with water. Bring to the boil, taking the scum off when it forms.
2. After about 35 minutes, when the lamb is almost cooked, add the chopped onion, spices and roughly chopped mint.
3. Very finely chop the apples and crush them with a mortar and add to the pot with the pre-soaked almonds.
4. Return the pan to the heat and add two chicken joints. Simmer until the chicken is cooked and serve with bread.

Veal Stew with Lamb Meatballs and Spinach

This is a really interesting recipe. You could always use chicken breasts if you don't eat veal.

250 g veal (or chicken breast) cut into cubes

50 g dripping

450 ml water

½ tsp salt

½ tsp ground coriander

½ tsp cumin

1 tsp cinnamon

¼ tsp pepper

Meatballs

225 g minced lamb

1 tsp cinnamon

1 tsp salt

½ tsp cumin

½ tsp coriander

1 finely chopped onion

450 g spinach leaves

3 cloves of garlic

Coriander and cinnamon to garnish

Method

1. Cut the veal into thin slices and brown in the dripping, then cover with water.

2. Bring to the boil and skim away any scum that forms.

3. Add the salt, coriander, cumin, pepper and cinnamon and continue cooking until the meat is tender.

4. To make the meatballs, add the minced lamb to the cinnamon, coriander, cumin and salt. Form into lots of small meatballs and put to one side.

5. Add the chopped spinach to the veal pan with the onion and garlic and stir well.

6. Put in the meatballs and bring the pot to the boil. Simmer until the meatballs are cooked and most of the liquid has evaporated. This might take about an hour.

7. Serve on a large platter and sprinkle with coriander and cinnamon.

Sweet and Sour Spicy Lamb

In this recipe we can clearly see the origins of the Medieval and Tudor obsession with spicy meat dishes that included dried fruit. Also, the equal quantity of honey and vinegar are the basis of any sweet and sour sauce, which we tend to think of as a Chinese invention.

1 kg breast of lamb

1 bunch fresh coriander

1 tbsp ground coriander

1 stick cinnamon

4 large onions

2 leeks

4 carrots

200 ml runny honey

200 ml vinegar

12 threads of saffron

½ tsp pepper

1 tsp cinnamon

125 g blanched almonds

50 g raisins

25 g currants

125 g dried figs

3 tbsp rose water

Method

1. Put the cubed meat, coriander (tied in a bunch), cinnamon stick and salt into a pan and cover with water.

2. Bring to the boil and remove the scum when it forms. Cook for 30 minutes.

3. Take the bunch of coriander out and add the dried coriander.

4. Into a separate pan, put the chopped onion, leek, carrot and salt with some water. Cook until tender and then strain.

5. Put these vegetables in with the meat in the first pan and add the rest of the ingredients and cook for about 15 minutes. Then mix the saffron with a little boiling water and add to the pot with the almonds and dried fruit. Cover the pot and put on a very low heat for another 15 minutes.

6. Serve in a large dish and sprinkle with rose-water.

Spinach with Spices

450 g spinach

1 tbsp sesame oil

2 cloves garlic, chopped finely

½ tsp cumin

½ tsp dry coriander

½ tsp cinnamon

1 tsp salt

Method

1. Cut off the stems and boil in a little salted water until cooked. Drain well.

2. Put the oil in a pan with the spices and garlic and cook for 1 minute, then stir in the spinach and serve at once.

Spiced Celery

1 tbsp sesame oil

300 g celery

½ tbsp dried coriander

1 tsp cumin

2 tbsp vinegar

A pinch of saffron

4 eggs

Method

1. Fry the chopped celery in the oil until tender.

2. Add the spices, vinegar and saffron and heat until hot.

3. Break the eggs individually into the pan, keeping them separate.

4. Put the lid on the pan and heat for 2 minutes until the eggs are cooked.

Sweet Fruit Cakes for Travellers

450 g breadcrumbs

450 g dates, stoned

125 g ground almonds

125 g pistachio nuts

225 g melted butter

Sugar to taste

Method

1. Add the melted butter to the chopped dates and nuts and gradually work in the bread-crumbs until you have a stiff dough.

2. Roll into balls and dust with icing sugar and store in a pot.

NB. These are great for taking on a walk and can be made into any shape you want. I wonder if the Crusaders took such sweetmeats with them into battle? They would certainly have given them an energy boost if they were flagging!

Sweet Almond-Filled Bread

This next recipe is just like my son's favourite Pashwari Naan bread that he orders with a takeaway curry!

500 g flour

150 ml oil

Water to mix

Filling

175 g ground almonds

350 g scented sugar (sugar that has been left in a jar for a week with a vanilla pod)

Rosewater to mix

Method

1. Make the dough by mixing the oil and flour and kneading it to a fine paste. If it is too dry, add a few tablespoons of water as necessary.

2. Leave the dough to rest in a warm place.

3. Make the filling by mixing the almonds with the sugar and moistening it with rosewater to make a paste.

4. Cut the dough into four pieces and roll out to a long, flat oblong piece.

5. Cut the dough in half lengthways and spread a quarter of the mixture along the middle of it.

6. Dampen the edges with water and place the other oblong piece on top, sealing it well all around the edge.

7. Bake on a tray in the oven until the bread is lightly browned – this should take about 15 minutes in a moderate oven.

Sweet and Sour Fish

This recipe clearly has its origins in the Crusaders' travels, as the sweet and sour sauce and the use of cloves are typical of Middle Eastern foods.

Sweet almond-filled bread. This is really very easy to make and goes well with curry or spicy food

1 kg haddock fillets

300 ml red wine vinegar

250 g sugar

1 onion, finely chopped

½ tsp mace

½ tsp cloves

1 tsp pepper

Method

1. Poach the fish in water and drain well.

2. Mix the vinegar with the sugar and onions and spices in a pan.

3. Bring the pan to the boil and simmer until the onion is soft.

4. Put the fish on a platter and ladle the boiling sauce over it and serve.

NB. The sauce should be hot enough to reheat the fish.

Saracen Brewet

Here is a recipe that actually has the word 'Saracen' in its name, so I think we can safely say it is a Crusader recipe.

900 g venison (can also be made using beef)

500 ml of almond milk, made with the stock from the boiled venison instead of water

1 onion

10 tbsp rice flour

6 cloves

½ tsp ginger

½ tsp cinnamon

2 tsp pepper

300 ml red wine

2 tbsp sugar

A few drops of red food colouring to replace sandalwood

2 tsp salt

Method

1. Put venison in a pan and cover with water. Boil until tender and drain, saving the stock.

2. Make the almond milk with the stock (400 ml stock to 125 g ground almonds).

3. Put in the almond milk, chopped onion and cloves, and heat until the onion is cooked.

4. Add the rice flour and cook until it has thickened, then add the wine, spices and red food colouring and heat through again for another 5 minutes.

5. Return the venison to the sauce and coat well before serving on a platter.

Barley Gruel

This would have been eaten for breakfast or as a snack by the rich in Norman times, as the almond milk would have been very expensive.

450 g pearl barley

2 litres of almond milk (made by mixing 2 litres of boiling water with 200 g ground almonds and straining it. The almonds can then be used in cakes or breads)

4 tbsp honey

½ tsp salt

Method

1. Soak the barley in water for 1 hour and strain. Put in a saucepan and just cover it with water. Bring to the boil and simmer with the lid on for 20 minutes until the grains become soft. Check every so often that it has not boiled dry, and if so, add more boiling water.

2. Strain and mash to a pulp.

3. In a pan bring the almond milk to the boil and add the mashed barley, stirring all the time until it boils again. Reduce the heat and add the salt and honey and simmer for 10 minutes.

4. Serve dotted with knobs of butter, and more honey if desired.

Frumenty

This is basically a wheat version of the barley gruel, using Bulgar wheat instead.

200 g Bulgar wheat

700 ml almond milk

3 saffron strands

½ tsp salt

Method

1. Put all the ingredients into a pan and bring to the boil.

2. Cover and simmer for 40 minutes or until the mixture is very thick and the liquid has been absorbed.

3. Serve with either honey or more salt for a savoury dish.

Mushroom Pie

This recipe is from early Medieval France, so it is likely that the Normans still ate it when they came to Britain.

450 g button mushrooms

2 tbsp olive oil

200 g chopped Brie or goats' cheese

1 tsp salt

½ tsp nutmeg

¼ tsp pepper

Pastry for pie

Method

1. Keep the mushrooms whole and boil them in salted water for 5 minutes, then leave in the water to soak (this makes the mushrooms nice and juicy).

2. Line the pie dish with pasty and add the drained mushrooms once they have been tossed in oil.

3. Cover with slices of cheese and sprinkle with nutmeg before putting on the pastry lid.

4. Bake in a moderate oven for 35 minutes or until the pastry is brown. Can be eaten either hot or cold.

Wild Blackberry and Wild Plum Crumble

The bounty of soft sweet wild fruits in the countryside would have been eagerly awaited at the end of the summer. All the ingredients in this recipe were readily available to even the lowliest villager in Norman Britain, and I am sure they would have made it. The poor would have had to cook it in a cauldron under a pot to form a primitive type of oven.

450 g blackberries

450 g wild plums (or chopped black plums)

150 g butter

75 g runny honey

200 g brown breadcrumbs

50 g toasted hazelnuts

Method

1. Chop the hazelnuts and add them to the breadcrumbs.

2. In a pan, melt the butter and honey together and pour onto the breadcrumbs and nuts and rub it through until well mixed.

3. Put the ripe sweet blackberries and stoned plums in a dish and top with the breadcrumb mix.

4. Bake in a hot oven for 30 minutes until nice and brown on top and the blackberry juices have risen up the sides of the dish.

5. Eat hot or cold with clotted cream (cream was clotted to make it last longer).

Vyolette

This is a lovely recipe, but only possible if you can get enough violet flowers. They grow wild in my valley so it is not a problem for me. You can buy them in lovely bunches in the markets in the spring too, but unfortunately, if you are not picking them from the wild or from your garden, you won't know if any pesticides have been used on them.

40 g violet petals

350 ml almond milk (made with 300 ml of water and 50 g ground almonds)

200 g water

6 tbsp sugar

3 tbsp rice flour

Method

1. Bring the water to the boil and add the violet petals. Return to the boil and cook for 1 minute.

2. Drain the petals and press out as much water as you can. Then chop them finely into a paste.

3. In a pan, heat the almond milk. Then reduce and simmer, stirring all the time for 2 minutes.

4. Add the violets to this and then the rice flour and the sugar.

5. Cook for another 5 minutes and serve.

NORMAN CHRISTMAS FEAST

The classic roast boar's head and roast goose and swan would have been the centrepieces of the Christmas dinner table in Norman castles.

Gode Paest

A rich pastry that can be made into decorative coats of arms and various other shapes on a feast day table.

450 g 100% wholemeal flour

50 g rice flour

75 g lard

75 g butter

50 g cream cheese

1 tsp salt

3 egg yolks

Water to mix

Method

1. Mix the two types of flour in one bowl and cream the fats together in a different bowl.

2. Add the fat to the flour and rub it in, then add the cheese, salt and egg yolks and work to a stiff pastry, adding a little water if it is too dry.

3. Leave to rest before rolling it into shapes, such as coats of arms or birds or fish to decorate the table.

4. Bake on a baking tray until firm to touch. These coats of arms could then be painted with food colouring and saffron before baking to make them more dramatic.

Stuffed Chicken Festive Style

This recipe calls for the whole chicken – with head, feet and all – to be taken out of its skin and stuffed and made to look like a bird again. It is then painted with bright colours to make it look very unnatural.

1 chicken with head and feet still attached (it would be best to get your butcher to do this)
500 g cooked pork or chicken, finely minced
6 eggs
150 g chestnuts
150 g breadcrumbs
150 g cream cheese
1 tsp cinnamon
½ tsp ginger
1 tsp savoury herb
1 tsp cumin
10 saffron threads
1 tsp salt
3 egg yolks
Yellow and red food colouring

Method

1. Mix the pork or chicken mince with the breadcrumbs, eggs, chestnuts, cheese, spices and herbs.
2. Stuff the bird with this mix, including part of the neck to keep the bird's head up when baked, and save four balls of the mix to make decorative eggs.
3. Roast the chicken for the required amount of time and when it is ready take it out of the oven, glaze its body with egg yolks and put back in the oven for a few seconds to set the glaze.
4. Take the bird out and paint the red and yellow food colouring on the head and feet and wings of the chicken.
5. While the chicken is in the oven roasting, cook the remaining stuffing in boiling water and then glaze with egg white and place in the oven for a few seconds to set.
6. Put the bird on a platter of green herbs and place its eggs on the herbs next to it.
NB. This must have been an extraordinary sight to see on any table!

Veal and Pork Pie

450 g pork
450 g veal
300 g currants
300 ml red wine
Stock made of pork and chicken stock cubes
200 g dates
8 egg yolks
1 tbsp sugar
1 tsp ginger
2 tsp salt
Hot water pastry (see page 68)

Method

1. Put the chopped pork and veal in a pot with the stock and wine and bring to the boil. Simmer until tender – this should take about 1 hour.
2. Let it cool a little and add the egg yolks, ginger, sugar, salt, minced dates and currants and mix well.
3. Pour this into a pastry case shaped by hand with the hot water crust pastry and top with a pastry lid.
4. Bake for 40 minutes in a moderate oven until the pastry is brown. Serve cold with salad.

Brie Tart

I am sure when the Normans arrived in Britain they would have made sure they were still able to get hold of their favourite cheeses, such as Brie. This Medieval British recipe shows that Brie was being made in Britain at the time, as I imagine that it would have been far too expensive to import.

6 eggs
500 g Brie, cut into pieces
½ tsp salt
10 threads of saffron
½ tsp ginger
Pastry case

Method

1. Beat the eggs, salt and saffron together and leave for 10 minutes for the saffron to infuse the eggs.

2. Sprinkle the base of the piecrust with ginger and top with the chopped Brie.

3. Cover with the egg mixture and bake in a moderate oven until set.

Cresses

This is an unusual sort of pasta dish with strips of pasta made into a lattice, half of which have been flavoured with cheese.

450 g flour

2 eggs

1 tsp salt

1 tsp ginger powder

2 tbsp sugar

20 threads saffron

1 tbsp boiling water

2 tbsp oil

75 g grated Parmesan cheese

Method

1. Put the saffron in a bowl and pour the boiling water over it.

2. Mix the ginger and sugar with half the flour, one egg, and half tsp salt and knead until it becomes a dough (add more water if necessary).

3. Strain the saffron and make another dough from the remaining flour, salt and egg.

4. When the saffron dough is soft, knead in the Parmesan until it is thoroughly mixed.

5. Roll the two doughs separately and cut into long finger-thickness strips.

6. Boil some water in two separate pans and cook the strips separately for 5 minutes.

7. When cooked, ladle out carefully and lay flat on a board to dry.

8. When cool enough to handle, make a chequerboard lattice on a baking tray using the two doughs.

9. Sprinkle with oil and bake in a moderate oven for 15 minutes.

10. Serve as a starter.

Fried Fig Tarts

The origins of this recipe must have come from the Roman period, because Apicius had a very similar recipe (see the chapter on the Romans).

250 g figs

100 ml honey

200 ml oil

1 egg

1 tsp cinnamon

1 tsp nutmeg

6 strands saffron

300 g pastry dough

Method

1. Chop the figs finely and mix them with the saffron and spices.

2. Roll out the pastry and cut into circles.

3. Add a spoonful of the mixture to the centre and moisten the edges. Put another circle of pastry on top.

4. Fry in hot oil on both sides until brown and crisp.

5. Serve on a dish and drizzle with the honey.

In addition to the above recipes, an exotic and special dessert during a Norman Christmas feast would simply have been bowls of dates, figs, apricots, raisins and pistachio nuts. These are incredibly sweet and would have been expensive, so they would have been eaten – as they were in the Middle East – as a dessert on their own.

THE MEDIEVAL PERIOD

The tables of the average Medieval noble-man was worlds apart from those of the serfs, just as they had been during the Norman period. The nobleman's table would have been brimming with beef, pork, veal, mutton, venison and game and a wide variety of fish. Rather than weak beer, they would have washed their food down with fine imported German and French table wines. To get an idea of this decadence, here is a menu for one of King Richard II's banquets:

Venison with a dish of boiled wheat
A Stewed Dish
A Boar's Head
A Roast Swan
Roasted Fat Capons
Peas and Pike
White Pudding
Jellied Meat and Fish
Roast Port with Crane and Heron
Pheasant
Tarts
Meat served in pieces
Roasted Rabbit
German Broth
Spiced pudding of pork and dried fruits
Eggs in a sauce of almond milk
Roasted Venison
Roasted Larks
Roasted Quails
Meat in puff pastry

Rice Dishes
Fruit Dumplings
Quince Puddings
Etc.

Table manners were not particularly refined at that time, and people would have eaten with their hands for the most part. Everyone brought their own knives and spoons with them when invited to the castle for dinner! If *this* banquet seems extravagant, just to give you an idea of the wealth and power of the Catholic Church at the time, take a look at the Archbishop of York's banquet menu below. It was a banquet given to celebrate his enthronement as Archbishop in AD 1466. One wonders just how many guests there were in the town to eat such a feast, and where on earth did they all sit?

300 loaves
104 oxen
6 wild bulls
1,000 sheep
304 calves
304 pigs
400 swans
2,000 geese
1,000 capons
400 plovers
100 dozen quail
104 peacocks
4,000 mallards

204 kids

2,000 chickens

4,000 pigeons

4,600 waterfowl of various sorts

200 pheasants

5,000 partridges

500 deer

4,000 cold venison pies

2,000 hot custards

608 pike

12 porpoises and seals

The menu also included an unspecified number of cakes and 300 tuns of ale and 1,000 tuns of wine. When I first saw this list, I thought someone had mistakenly added a lot of 'o's to the figures! How did they cook it all? And how many plates would be needed to display it all, let alone eat it? Well, all you can say for sure is that the Archbishop of York must have been a pretty important person at the time!

Fish also became a widespread foodstuff in the Medieval period due to the power of the Church, as it forbade the eating of meat on Saturdays, Wednesdays and Fridays. In the later Middle Ages, this was limited to just Fridays, and is still adhered to by practicing Catholics today. As you can image, that meant a lot of fish consumption in the country as a whole, far more than the local rivers could provide for inland. So monasteries and stately homes had fish ponds specially made in order to supply them with fish three times a week.

As you saw on the King's menu, roasted rabbits were of the same culinary status as roasted swans. In the twelfth century the Normans introduced the rabbit to Britain, and by the Medieval period they were still exclusively a food for the rich. The Medieval name for rabbit was 'Conay', which we still use today for the fur of the rabbit. Rabbits were carefully bred in warrens under the watch of the Warrener. The largest rabbit-breeding centre in Britain was at a town called Becks, in Suffolk. It is thought

that the dry, sandy soil there was easy for the rabbits to make and establish their large burrows in. The Warrener of the Abbey of Ealy in 1251 was said to be the highest paid manorial official in the land because of the importance of rabbit meat to the Abbot at the time.

By contrast to all this lavish food was the food of the farm labourer and serf. His food was as plain and simple as the Archbishop of York's feast was ridiculously extravagant.

The farm labourer would rise before dawn and eat some rye bread and water. Then at midday he would return home for lunch, which was bread again, but this time with cheese and watery beer (our typical ploughman's lunch). In the evening, when it was too dark to work outside, he would have some thick vegetable soup with salt meat and perhaps once a week he would eat some fish caught from the local river. Not too far removed, then, from the diet of the Norman or Saxon peasants.

During this period, every large village and town had a communal cook shop. This was more than just a local bakery. They did make and sell a wide selection of baked meats, pies and puddings, but what was unusual was that – for a small fee – you could add your own pies or roasts to their oven, as most people did not have their own oven at home. People walking about in a Medieval village or town street would therefore very often be seen carrying large baskets of steaming hot food back to their homes. It must have been terrible for those who could not afford more than a bowl of vegetable and barley broth to smell roast chicken and pork in the streets every day.

Bread, however, was everyone's staple food, both rich and poor alike, although the bread eaten by the poor was very different from that eaten by their Lord in his castle. The reason for this was the type of soil and work involved to grow the different grains that the bread was made from. Bread wheat needs good, fertile soil to grow a good crop, and this was always owned by the Lord of the manor. The quality bread they made from this wheat was called Pandemain, and was made from wheat flour that was sifted more than twice to make it white.

Conversely, most peasants ate Maslin, which was a dark brown bread made from a mixture of wheat and rye grains. Peasants in the north and the west of Britain ate oat and barley bread because those grains grew better in the wetter climates. It is ironic that, today, oat and barley breads are sold in fancy bakeries in Knightsbridge for the very rich, and the plain white bread, which was only for the tables of the nobility, is now eaten by the poorest people in our country.

In the towns, Medieval cooking relied on strong flavourings to improve the taste of dubious food, especially meat kept in larders that were rarely clean or cool in the summer months. Washing the meat with vinegar was the most common suggestion in the cookbooks of the time, but the use of spices to mask the smell of tainted meats was the most highly recommended. Housewives would grow a wide selection of herbs in their small gardens with which to season their food, and added to those herbs would be a generous amount of garlic, salt and mustard seeds to mask the taste of over-ripe meat and fish.

TYPICAL MEDIEVAL FOOD INGREDIENTS

Almond Milk

The typical uses of almonds in the Medieval period could be taken directly from the ancient Baghdad manuscript: 'Take a portion of sweet almonds, peel, grind fine, stir in water and add to the pan. Make a broth as desired of the milk of the almond.' You can make it in various strengths; the most common was to steep 100 g ground almonds in 400 ml of boiling water and

strain before use. The strained nuts could then be used in cakes.

This almond milk was used in Britain in stews with various combinations of different spices. Almond milk was only used by the nobility though, as you can imagine. It was very much enjoyed by the clergy at the time as a milk substitute, needed during times of church fasting when milk and butter products were forbidden. The Baghdad manuscript also described how to make marzipan shapes into fish, cocks and lambs, etc. by using wooden moulds. This fashion of making marzipan figures was a typical end to any grand banquet in the Medieval and later historical periods.

Candied Peel

This method of preserving the flavour of oranges and lemons in an easily transportable form was thought to have been developed in Arab-controlled Spain. Candied orange and lemon peel was exported from there to France and England during that period; it was called 'succade'. Once sugar became more available, the stems of one of our most common marsh plants – Angelica – were candied in Britain. This green sweet was a delight to those who wanted to add colour to their desserts, along with the candied orange and lemon peels.

Verjuice

This was an acidic ingredient to counteract the sweetness of a dish. It was made from the juice of sour grapes or apples, but you could use cider vinegar in equal quantities with water or, as an alternative, lime juice or lemon juice with equal parts of water.

Sanders

This was primarily a food colouring derived from sandalwood. Red food colouring could be used as an alternative instead, as there may be toxins in sandalwood today.

Gode Broth

This is mentioned in a lot of Medieval recipes, and it is made from the roasted bones of chicken and pork. It is much easier to just use a combination of chicken and pork stock cubes in boiling water for these recipes.

Saffron

This was used a lot in Medieval food to give it that bright yellow colour and distinct flavour. It is easy enough to come by today, so I would use it rather than yellow food colouring. Lots of saffron yellow-coloured and sanders red-coloured dishes were served on the same table to make them look bright and appealing.

Powder Fort

This was used in lots of Medieval recipes, and is a hot spice mix.

½ tbsp ground cloves

½ tbsp mace

2 tsp ground ginger

2 tbsp cinnamon

2 tbsp black pepper

Scale down this mix if you are not planning to do a lot of Medieval cooking.

Powder Douce

This was the other favourite spice mix, but this one is sweet.

1 tbsp fennel seeds

1 tbsp aniseed

1 tbsp cinnamon

1 tbsp crushed cardamom pods

4 tbsp sugar

Grind all the above in a pestle and mortar and store in a jar in the fridge until use. This powder used to contain Hyssop, which is now known to have some nasty side effects for some people and so I have left it out. The fennel and aniseed give it enough flavour anyway.

Gode Powder

1 tbsp cinnamon

1 tbsp mace

½ tbsp nutmeg

1 tsp pepper

1 tbsp crushed cardamom

1 tbsp galingale

This is a really good sweet mixed spice, but unfortunately galingale, which has a violet sort of flavour, is no longer available. It is made from the root of a sedge grass and is no longer harvested in this country for its culinary uses. It has such a delicate flavour, though, that I don't think it will be missed in this gode powder recipe.

Frumente

This was one of the most common Medieval side dishes.

450 g wheat grain

600 ml gode stock (made with 1 chicken and 1 pork stock cube, with 1 tsp cumin added to it)

300 ml almond milk

3 egg yolks

1 tbsp saffron

1 tbsp salt

Method

1. Boil the wheat in water until it bursts. Drain it and let it cool.

2. Mix the broth with the almond milk and wheat together in a big saucepan.

3. Bring it slowly to the boil, and then reduce the heat.

4. Simmer, stirring every so often for another 20 minutes.

5. Stir in the egg yolk, saffron and salt to taste and keep cooking on a low heat for a few more minutes, stirring all the time.

6. When it is thick like porridge, it is ready. It can be eaten with meat, or just on its own.

Medieval Dish of Chickpeas

2 tins of chickpeas (you can used dried, but it takes so much longer and tastes no better)

3 cloves of garlic

2 tbsp olive oil

3 threads of saffron (steeped in 2 tbsp boiling water)

1 tbsp powder fort

1 tsp salt

Method

1. Drain the chickpeas and put them onto a baking sheet. Place into a hot oven for 15 minutes, turning half way through the cooking time. (The original recipe says to put the chickpeas in the ashes of a fire to roast them, which is why I suggest that they should be baked, and not just pulverised from the tin.)

2. When they are roasted, use either a mortar or a food processor and add the other ingredients, including the strained saffron.

3. If too dry, add more oil and serve with bread.

Tart for Fast Day

2 large onions

1 bunch parsley

225 g green cheese (such as sage cheese)

2 tbsp melted butter

4 threads saffron

1½ tsp gode powder

50 g raisins

6 eggs

1 pastry case, baked blind

Method

1. Chop the parsley and the onions together and boil them in water for 10 minutes.

2. Grate the cheese and beat the eggs, adding the gode powder and the salt.

3. Drain the onions and dry well. Add to the other ingredients.

4. Pour into the pastry shell and bake in a moderate oven for 35 minutes or until it is set and firm to the touch.

Mushroom and Cheese Pies

450 g button mushrooms

2 tbsp oil

300 g strong cheddar cheese, grated

¼ tsp pepper

¼ tsp ground nutmeg

Salt to taste

Pastry

Method – filling

1. Wash the mushrooms and boil them in water for 1 minute.

2. Leave to stand in the water for 15 minutes.

3. Drain mushrooms and fry in the oil until browned.

4. Sprinkle with pepper and nutmeg and salt to taste.

5. Add the grated cheese and stir in the pan until it has melted into the mushrooms.

Method – pastry

1. Mix 450 g brown flour with 225 g of lard in a bowl.

2. Add 1 tsp salt and enough water to mix into dough.

3. Chill for 1 hour.

4. Roll out and line a small dish.

5. Fill with mushroom and cheese mixture and top with pastry.

6. Brush the pie with egg and sprinkle some grated cheese and nutmeg on top.

7. Bake in a moderate oven for 35 minutes until the pastry is golden. This is good hot or cold.

Cabbage Stew

1 Savoy cabbage

2 large onions

4 strands saffron steeped in 1 tbsp boiling water

1 tbsp powder douce

600 ml beef stock

Method

1. Shred the cabbage and chop the onions and cover with beef stock.

2. Bring to the boil and turn down the heat. Then add the saffron.

3. Simmer for 30 minutes until soft and until

most of the liquid has evaporated.

4. Put into large dishes, sprinkle with the douce powder and serve.

Watercress and Cheese Supper Dish

There are two versions of this dish, depending on whether or not it is to be eaten on a fast day.

1 large bunch of watercress

1 handful of chard or spinach leaves

Chicken stock (for meat day version only)

250 g cheese (for meat day version only)

2 tbsp oil (or 25 g butter for meat day version)

Salt to taste

Method – fast day version

1. Bring a pan of water to the boil add the cress and chard and cook until tender.

2. Remove from the heat and allow it to drain thoroughly.

3. When completely dry, chop the cress and chard into small pieces.

4. Heat the oil in a large pan and add the cress and chard to it.

5. Fry until the leaves are just browned.

6. Remove from the heat and drain well. Season with salt and serve.

Method – meat day version

1. Bring a pan of chicken stock to the boil and add the cress and chard and cook until tender.

2. Remove from the heat and allow it to drain thoroughly.

3. Add 2 tbsp butter to the frying pan and cook the drained cress and chard until lightly browned.

4. Add the grated cheese and toss in the pan to mix with the leaves. Add a little salt and serve.

Minted Mackerel with Sorrel Sauce

Fish was very popular during the Medieval period, as meat was forbidden for so many days of the week.

3 medium-sized mackerel

1 large bunch fresh mint

1 large bunch fresh parsley

1 tsp salt

1 bunch sorrel (wild, if you can get it)

Salt and pepper to taste

Method

1. Clean the mackerel well.

2. Bring a big pan of water to the boil with the salt in it.

3. Put the mint and parsley bunches in it and then put the fish on top of them.

4. Simmer for 30 minutes until the fish is cooked.

5. Put the herbs from the pan on a platter and lay the fish on top.

6. Add 300 ml of the stock with the sorrel in a pan and cook for 5 minutes.

7. Season with salt and pepper and pour over the fish.

Pickled Fish

1 kg fish (either salmon, cod, haddock, turbot or plaice)

300 ml vinegar

300 ml wine

½ tsp pepper

1 pinch saffron

Method

1. Put the wine, vinegar, pepper and saffron in a saucepan.

2. Add the fish and simmer for a further 10 minutes or until the fish is cooked.

3. Take the fish out of the pan and put it in a bowl.

4. Strain the stock and pour over the fish. Leave overnight.

5. Serve cold with salad or bread.

Tart of Pickled Fish

50 g figs

50 g raisins

4 apples, peeled and chopped

3 pears, peeled and chopped

300 ml wine

50 g sugar

250 g pickled fish

¼ tsp ginger

¼ tsp nutmeg
½ tsp cinnamon
1 tsp salt
Pastry shell for dish
5 prunes
5 dates
5 plums
Method
1. Mince the figs, raisins, apples and pears together.
2. Chop the fish into pieces and mix with the wine and sugar.
3. Mix in the spices and salt and put in a pan to cook for 15 minutes.
4. Leave to cool and put in the pastry case.
5. Arrange the prunes, dates and plums over the top of the tart and bake in a moderate oven for 35 minutes.
6. Serve cold with salad

Spiced Rabbit

Don't forget that this would still have been an expensive and exotic meat at the time.
500 g rabbit, cut into pieces
2 large onions
1 handful of raisins
125 g lard
300 ml red wine
3 tbsp sugar
3 tbsp red wine vinegar
½ tsp pepper
1 tsp cinnamon
1 tsp ground ginger
1 tsp salt (add more if you like)
Method
1. Parboil the onions and then chop them finely.
2. Fry the rabbit in half the lard until browned.
3. When browned, add the raisins and cook for a further 5 minutes.
3. Add the rest of the lard and the onions and cook for 5 minutes.
4. Put the contents of the pan into a casserole dish.

5. Into the pan, put the spices and the wine, sugar and vinegar and stir until all the meat juices have been taken up.
6. Pour this over the rabbit and cook in a slow oven for 4 hours (if you have a slow cooker, that would be perfect).
7. Serve with chunks of bread to soak up the rich gravy.

SWEET DISHES

Pokerounce or Honey Toasts

225 g thick clover honey
A pinch of cinnamon, ginger and black pepper
Four slices of white bread, with the crusts cut off
A handful of pine kernels
Method
1. Put the honey, spices and pepper into a small pan and gently heat until the honey melts.
2. Simmer gently for 1 minute.
3. Toast the bread and cut it into shapes.
4. Put the bread shapes onto a heatproof dish and pour over the honey and spices.
5. Decorate the bread shapes with pine kernels stuck in upright.
6. Put the dish in the oven for 5 minutes to heat through and serve.

Leche Lumbard or Date Slices

1 kg stoned dates (make sure they really are stoned by cutting each in half with a knife)
450 ml dry white wine
4 oz brown sugar
½ tsp cinnamon
½ tsp ginger
6 hard-boiled egg yolks
6 oz soft brown breadcrumbs
4 tbsp Madeira wine heated with a pinch of mixed spice (if you don't have Madeira, just use sherry with a little brown sugar in it)
Method
1. Put the dates and sugar in a pan with the wine and simmer gently until pulpy.

2. Mix in the spices and work in the cooked, sieved egg yolks.

3. When cool, knead in a bowl until smooth and the consistency of marzipan.

4. Form into a long sausage shape and chill.

5. When cold, cut into thin disks and lay them on a serving dish.

6. Sprinkle the disks with the Madeira spiced wine and serve.

NB. These disks can be covered in edible gold leaf for a very special sweet.

Sweet Cheese Flan

150 g flour

75 g lard (to make the pastry case, rub the fat and flour together and line a deep dish, then bake it blind)

A pinch of saffron

1 tbsp boiling water

350 g Brie (without the rind)

4 egg yolks

50 g fine sugar

A pinch ginger

A pinch salt

Method

1. Soak the saffron in the boiling water until a deep golden colour.

2. Beat the cheese (without the rind) in a bowl until light and creamy.

3. Beat the egg yolks and sugar together until pale.

4. Add the softened cheese a little at a time until all is mixed together.

5. Add the ginger, salt and saffron water and mix well.

6. Put mixture into the pastry case and bake in a medium oven for 30 minutes or until set in the centre.

NB. This is best eaten cold the next day and decorated with rose or primrose petals.

Bread Pudding

1 loaf of stale white bread

2 glasses of red wine

225 g honey

225 g raisins

125 g candied peel

150 g melted butter

4 tbsp water

3 egg whites lightly beaten

½ tsp mace

½ tsp gode powder

¼ clove powder

¼ tsp salt

Method

1. Cut the bread into cubes and fry in butter until they are golden.

2. Into a pan, put the honey, egg whites and water and bring to the boil, skimming off the scum.

3. Remove from the heat and put it in a bowl with the fried bread cubes.

4. Add the spices, salt, raisins, ginger, honey and red wine.

5. Mix well, and if the mixture is too stiff, add more wine. If it is too wet, add more bread.

6. Put in an ovenproof dish and bake for 30 minutes in a cool oven until it is just browned on top. This can be served either hot or cold.

Almond Milk Fruit Pie

600 ml almond milk

50 g chopped dates

2 sweet apples, peeled, cored and chopped

2 sweet pears, peeled, cored and chopped

125 g pitted prunes, sliced thinly

50 g currants

50 g sugar

½ tsp cinnamon

½ tsp mace

2 tsp gode powder

¼ tsp salt

Red food colouring (instead of sanders)

2 tbsp olive oil

Pastry lined dish

Method

1. Put in a bowl the almond milk, sugar, spices, oil and food colouring. The mixture should be thick.

2. In another bowl, mix together the fruit. Add the almond milk mixture to it and mix well.

3. Put it in the pie dish and bake in a moderate oven for 45 minutes or until set and light brown.

4. Remove from the oven and allow to cool completely before serving.

Cherry Pudding (Chyryse)

100 g ground almonds
500 g fresh cherries
150 ml sweet white wine
Water if needed to thin the batter
3 slices of white bread
½ tsp cinnamon
½ tsp ginger
Salt to taste
Method

1. Put the ground almonds in a bowl with the spices, the wine and the beaten egg and mix well.

2. Add enough water to make a thick batter-like consistency.

3. Pit the cherries and halve them and save a handful for decoration.

4. Fold the cherries into the batter in the bowl.

5. Add the spices and gently heat the mixture over a low heat for 5 minutes. Then remove from the heat.

6. Cover the bottom of a serving dish with cubes of white bread and spoon the cherry mixture over the top.

7. Decorate with the cherries and serve either hot or cold.

MEDIEVAL CHRISTMAS

This makes a great starter:

Toasted Bread with Almond Milk and Onions (Sops Dorroy)

2 onions, sliced
1 tbsp olive oil

1 tsp salt
150 ml red wine
1 loaf of white bread
150 ml almond milk
Method

1. Fry the onions in the oil until tender and add the red wine. Simmer for 10 minutes to reduce.

2. Cut the loaf into thick slices and toast on both sides. Arrange the toast on a platter.

3. Spoon the almond milk over the toast evenly and then top with the onions in red wine sauce.

4. Serve immediately.

Roast Goose with Stuffing

3 kg goose
1 tbsp sage
2 tbsp parsley
1 tbsp savoury
3 pears
3 quinces (if you can get them – if not, use more pears)
2 cloves garlic
225 g grapes
1 tsp salt
Method

1. Mix all the above ingredients together and stuff the goose with it.

2. Sew up the cavity with string tightly to keep in all the stuffing, and roast the goose in the usual way.

3. Serve with fried beans and onions and the rich stock from the pan that has been reduced.

Fried Herbs

This is really nice served on a platter to nibble while you are waiting for your feast. You can use any combination of herbs, but here is a recipe I particularly like.

1 bunch of parsley
1 sprig of rosemary
A handful of sage
A sprig of thyme
A handful of marjoram
125 g flour

Zest of a lemon

Oil for frying

4 tbsp honey to drizzle with

1 tsp salt

Method

1. Chop the herbs, taking away any stems, and mix with the flour, salt and lemon zest.

2. Add enough water to make a stiff batter.

3. Fry spoonfuls of the mixture in hot oil, turning once to brown them.

4. Put on a platter and drizzle with honey.

NB. I like to put them on two platters: one with honey drizzled on it and one with salt sprinkled on it.

Pork Oranges

Here is an interesting and quite elaborate dish to create a fancy effect on the table, but I doubt this sort of thing would have been made every day.

450 g minced pork

6 egg yolks

1 tsp salt

¼ tsp pepper

3 egg whites, lightly beaten

1 litre stock made with 1 chicken and 1 pork stock cube

1 tbsp sugar

Method

1. Mix the minced pork with 3 egg yolks and salt and pepper.

2. Roll into balls with your hands and coat in egg white.

3. Make a broth with the stock cubes and bring it to the boil. Gently add the pork balls.

4. After 10 minutes take the pork balls out and drain them.

5. Put the balls on a baking tray and cook in a moderate oven until they just start to go brown – this should take about 10–15 minutes.

6. Take them out of the oven and coat with egg white, then return to the oven for 40 seconds to dry the egg white.

7. Take out again and brush with egg yolk.

Return once more to the oven to dry for about another 30 seconds.

8. Sprinkle with sugar and serve.

NB. When the pork oranges are cut open, the edge should look like the white of the pith and the orange peel. As I said, a lot of trouble to go to, so I would imagine that this would only have been made on feast days.

White Chicken Pottage

Here is a delicious white dish to be served with those pork oranges:

1 chicken

2 onions

2 leeks (cut off all the green parts)

Chicken stock (from the bones of your chicken)

2 tbsp sugar

1 tsp powder douce

3 saffron strands

1 tsp salt

Method

1. Roast your chicken in the usual way and take off all the meat.

2. Add water and salt to the bones of the chicken and make a stock with it by simmering for 2 hours. Drain and discard the bones.

3. Wash the leeks and cut them finely in long strands, using only the white part. Chop the onions finely too, and put them into the stock. Simmer until they are tender.

4. Add the shredded chicken meat to the pot and simmer until all the water has evaporated.

5. Stir in the sugar and the powder douce and 1 tsp salt.

6. Pour the chicken and onion pottage into a large dish and put the saffron strands in the middle, so that the saffron will leach colour into the middle of the plate of white food.

Pears in Spiced Red Wine

This is almost identical to the modern version.

6 pears, peeled

500 ml red wine

100 ml port

200 g mulberries (or use blueberries if you can't get them)

400 g sugar

1 tsp cloves

2 tsp cinnamon

Method

1. Soak the pears in the wine with the port and berries for 3 hours.

2. Take the pears out of the liquid and put them on a plate.

3. Add the sugar and spices and slowly bring to the boil. Simmer for 1 hour until you have a light syrup.

4. Return the pears to the pan and simmer them slowly for another hour.

5. Let them cool in a bowl full of syrup and serve with cream.

Roasted Fruits (for snacks)

6 fresh figs, quartered

200 g raisins (the very big ones)

100 g whole pitted dates (usually only available at Christmas)

100 g blanched almonds

4 tbsp olive oil

Method

1. Put all the above in a bowl and toss in the oil until well coated.

2. Put on a baking tin and heat in a moderate oven for about 4 minutes. Then turn everything and cook for another 5 minutes.

3. Put into a dish and serve as a tasty snack.

Parsnip, Carrot and Apple Fritters

This recipe is from the fourteenth century and is a great snack to serve with drinks before dinner.

500 g flour

1 egg

300 ml beer

1 parsnip

2 carrots

6 cooking apples

Method

1. Peel and core the apples, parsnips and carrots and chop into small cubes.

2. Put in a pan and cover with water. Boil until cooked and then drain.

Pears in spiced red wine. This is one of my most favourite desserts smothered with thick west country cream

Parsnip, carrot and apple fritters, I was not sure what these would be like when I first found the recipe, but they are so good I have now made them many times as a sort of starter at a BBQ as you can cook them on a hot plate. Sprinkle them with salt crystals just before serving

3. Mash well with a fork.

4. In a bowl, mix the flour, egg and beer to make a stiff batter.

5. Add the mashed vegetables and mix well.

6. Heat the oil in a pan until it is very hot and drop spoonfuls of the batter into it. Cook on both sides until golden.

7. Serve at once sprinkled with salt. If they go cold, reheat them in the oven before serving.

DRINK

Wassail

1½ lb apples, cored

1 quart ale

1 tablespoon (or more) of sugar

¼ tsp ground ginger

¼ tsp nutmeg

Method

1. Preheat oven to 375 degrees.

2. Bake the apples in a large dish for 45 minutes, or until they burst.

3. Set them aside to cool.

4. When the apples are cool enough to handle, remove the peel and mash the pulp. You should have about 1½ cups.

5. In a large pot, heat the ale and whisk and blend in the apple pulp, sugar and spices. Adjust the seasonings to taste.

6. Place the mixture in a heatproof bowl ready for ladling out and sprinkle the top with some additional nutmeg.

THE ELIZABETHANS

When I think of the Elizabethan period, I think of small ships being given unofficial licence by the Queen to plunder Spanish galleons laden with gold from South America. At the same time, I think about the regrettable arrival to our shores of the potato and the tobacco leaf. There is nothing wrong with the potato, of course, except for my part that I love it a little too much for the good of my hips! As for the tobacco leaf, I don't think I need to talk about that!

To give you an indication of the food of the common people in the Elizabethan period, we have a poem by Thomas Tusser – a poet, musician and farmer at the time who wrote a book called *100 Points of Good Husbandry*, published in 1557. 'A fool and his money are soon parted', was one of his sayings, and one that is still quoted today. He wrote the following poem about a farmer's daily diet throughout the year. It ends with yet another famous quote about Christmas that we still use today, 'Christmas comes but once a year.'

A plot set down, for farmers quiet,
As time requires, to farm his diet;
With sometime fish and sometime fast,
That household store, may longer last.

Let Lent well kept offend not this,
For March and April breeders be,
Spend Herring, first souse, salt fish last,
For salt fish is good when lent is past.

When Easter comes, who knows not than,
That veal and bacon is the man,
And Mittlemas beef doth bare good tack,
When countries folk do dainties lack.

When mackerel ceases from the seas,
John Baptist brings fresh beef and peas,
Fresh herring plenty, Mihell brings
With fatted Crones [mutton] and such old things.

All saints do lay for pork and souse [pickled pork],
For sprats and spurlings for the house,
At Christmas lay and make good cheer,
For Christmas comes but once a year.

At the other end of the scale, there were the newly imported foods from the New World being cooked in the kitchens of the rich, no doubt by a number of rather bemused cooks! That new produce from the New World really added the last of the ingredients that we eat on our tables today. We imagine the Elizabethans delighting when they tried some of the ingredients listed below, but a lot were viewed with more than a little superstition. Tomatoes were definitely thought to be suspect, and it was not until the Victorian period, when they started to make chutneys and ketchups, that the popularity of the tomato really took off. Here is a list of the foods imported at the time: tomatoes, sweet corn, kidney beans, lima beans, pumpkins, avocado, red peppers, squash, tapioca, peanuts, pecan nuts, cashew nuts, chilli, pineapples, coffee, chocolate and, of course, the turkey – and where would Christmas dinner be without that now?

As I said previously, these new foods were only for the very rich in Elizabethan Britain. Sugar was so prized, even though they knew it rotted their teeth, that it actually became fashionable among the less fortunate to cosmetically blacken their teeth!

The diet of the rich Elizabethan was, however, poor for many other reasons too. The rich ate very few fresh vegetables or fresh fruit, as unprepared or uncooked fruit and vegetables were viewed with some suspicion. The favourite cooked vegetables seen on the tables of the gentry was garlic, onions and leeks. Dairy products were also looked on as inferior foodstuffs and were consequently left for the poor. The rich only drank milk as a beverage, and would only eat butter when it was used in cooking. The fine array of cheeses, curds and whey products they made at the time were never eaten in their natural state. The bread of the rich was called Manchet – a fine white bread made out of double-sieved flour.

So if you think about it, the peasants were eating stews made with lots of fresh vegetables, and were eating the fresh fruit they grew in their gardens. They ate wholemeal bread with butter and cheese for lunch and by our modern standards, we would look on that as a fine diet. Honey was also thought of as a food for the lower classes. The farmer would maybe eat a fresh apple from his orchard for a snack while the noble Lord in his castle would snack on gingerbread and marzipan instead. Being very overweight, like Elizabeth I's father, Henry the VIII, became almost a status symbol at the court during those times.

A writer in 1577 described a particular Elizabethan banquet as follows:

On the table was placed a centre piece, which represented a green lawn surrounded with larch trees made of peacock's feathers and green branches, to which were tied bunches of violets and other sweet smelling flowers. In the middle of the lawn a fortress was placed covered with silver. This was hollow and formed a sort of cage in which several live birds were shut up with gilded feet.

First course
At both ends of the lawn was an enormous pie surmounted with smaller pies to form a crown and the crust of the large one was silvered all around it and gild on the top. Each pie contained a whole roe deer, a gosling, three capons, six chickens, ten pigeons and a rabbit. To go with the pie was a stuffing of minced loin of veal with two pounds of fat and twenty-six hard-boiled eggs covered with cloves. [That's what I call a large pie!]

Second course
A roe deer, a pig, a sturgeon cooked with parsley and vinegar and sprinkled with powdered ginger, a kid, two goslings, twelve chickens and many pigeons, rabbits, two herons, a fat stuffed capon and four chickens covered with egg yolks and sprinkled with spice powder and a wild boar.

Third course
Wafers (darioles) and stars and a jelly part white and part red representing the crest of their guests.

Fourth course
Cream covered with fennel seeds and sugar, a white cream and strawberries and lastly plums stewed in rose water.

Fifth course
Besides the four courses there was a fifth entirely composed of prepared wines that

were in vogue and preserves. These consisted of fruits and various sweet pastries, the pastries represented stags and swans to the necks of which were suspended the coats of arms of the Count of Anjou.

If this was a typical banquet at the palace of the Queen, I am sure many would not have had a problem becoming fashionably overweight! The tableware was also becoming extremely elaborate, being made of ceramic, pewter, glass, silver and gold. The fashion was also to have fine Venetian glass goblets, rather than silver goblets.

At the same time, the average person would not eat from a plate at all. He would eat from a slab of bread called a trencher, just as they had done in the Medieval period. The easiest way to make such a platter is to buy a loaf and slice it in half sideways, scooping out the breadcrumbs so that you have two nice crust-edged bowls to serve your stew or pottage in. You could then eat the gravy-soaked dish later that day if you were too full to manage it straight away after the stew.

Pottage with Whole Herbs

Vegetables were called herbs at the time.
500 g mutton, veal or goat
A handful of oatmeal
1 lettuce
A good bowl of spinach
1 small endive
1 chicory
1 cauliflower
2 small onions
½ tsp salt
2 tbsp wine vinegar
6 slices of toast
Method
1. Add the meat whole to a large stockpot and pour over just enough water to cover it.
2. Bring the water to the boil, skim off any excess scum and add the vegetables whole with all the other ingredients.

3. Lower the heat to a simmer and keep cooking slowly for 1 hour. Check the pot frequently and skim off any surface fat as it cooks.
4. To serve, pour the liquid into a bowl, take the meat out and break it into strips. Add this to the liquid with the chopped vegetables.
5. Toast the brown bread and chop into pieces and drop on top of the pottage. More bread can be served with this dish to soak up the gravy.
NB. Any liquid from the bowl of pottage not soaked up with the bread would be drunk from the bowl itself.

Pease Pottage (Elizabethan style)

This can be served hot with bread or cold on a slice of bread. You can cut it into blocks and fry it in butter the next day, or add ham or fried bacon to it. These are the quantities in the original recipe, so they were either having a party or eating it in various ways all week!
1 kg dried peas (soaked overnight)
1 handful of coriander seeds, crushed
1 large onion
A bunch of mint
A bunch of winter savoury
A bunch of marjoram
A bunch of parsley
250 g butter
Salt and pepper to taste
Method
1. Cover the peas in lots of water and bring to the boil. Cook until they are soft.
2. Take out half the peas and strain them (these are kept whole).
3. To the pot, add the coriander crushed well and the finely chopped herbs and onion.
4. Bring the pot to the boil and cook for a further 30 minutes until the herbs have released their flavour and the onions are cooked.
5. Drain and push through a strainer.
6. Return the whole peas to the pot with the puréed peas and add the butter, salt and pepper to taste.

Elizabethan Pease Pottage in trencher bread. This is great to serve in scooped out crusty rolls as a winter starter

7. Stir over a low heat until the butter has melted and serve with crusty bread and perhaps some fried bacon.

Cucumber Pudding

This is an unusual dish, and very tasty too.

1 cucumber (nice and fat if possible)
1 lamb's liver
50 g green grapes
75 g breadcrumbs
1 tsp salt
¼ tsp pepper
25 g suet
¼ tsp cloves
3 egg yolks
300 ml mutton stock or a lamb stock cube and water
1 tbsp vinegar
50 g butter
Cubes of bread without the crusts from half a loaf

Method

1. Slice the top off the cucumber lengthways and scoop out the contents, leaving 1 cm of flesh.
2. Chop the liver and the grapes and mix together with the breadcrumbs, spices, seasoning, egg yolks and suet. This should be a nice stiff stuffing.
3. Stuff the cucumber and put the top slice back in place, tying well with string.
4. In an oven proof dish, put the bread cubes at the base and settle the cucumber amongst them, supporting it to keep it upright.
5. Make the stock up to 1 litre with boiling water and add the butter and vinegar to it.
6. Slowly pour the stock onto the bread cubes. Bake in a moderate oven for at least 1 hour

until all the stock has evaporated, the cucumber is tender and the bread cubes are beginning to crisp.

7. Serve on a platter and cut into slices.

Hard-Boiled Eggs in Mustard Sauce

4 hard-boiled eggs

100 g butter

4 tsp English Mustard (homemade)

4 tsp vinegar

½ tsp salt

¼ tsp pepper

Method

1. Boil the eggs and peel them and cut into quarters.

2. Melt the butter in a pan until it starts to become brown.

3. Add the other ingredients, stirring all the time. When combined, take off the heat.

4. Put the eggs on a plate and cover with the mustard sauce.

Great Grand Salad

A handful each of the following:

Young leaves of a lettuce

Sorrel

Mustard

Watercress

Dandelion

Spinach

1 bunch of radishes

500 g green cabbage

225 g capers

12 dates, stoned and split lengthwise

60 g currants

60 g raisins

60 g blanched almonds

6 figs, thinly sliced

6 mandarin oranges, peeled and segmented

For the Decoration

5 small sprigs of rosemary

4 small lemons

250 g fresh cherries (with stems)

6 hard-boiled eggs

Method

1. Toss together the ingredients of the salad in a large bowl (but reserve half the capers, dates, almonds and orange segments for decoration).

2. Arrange the leaves across the bottom of a wide, shallow dish.

3. Meanwhile, spear the rosemary sprigs into the pointed ends of five half lemons and hang it with pairs of cherries.

4. Place one in the middle of the dish and arrange the others around the edge. Slice four eggs lengthways and stick the reserved almonds and dates into these before arranging them between the half lemons.

5. Quarter the remaining lemons and eggs and arrange in an alternating pattern around the rim of the bowl.

6. Finally, place the remaining orange segments around the very edge of the bowl's rim. Sprinkle the capers on top and serve.

Salad of all Kinds of Herbs and Flowers

1 bunch sheep's sorrel

1 bunch watercress

1 bunch chives

1 bunch young dandelion leaves

2 tbsp chopped mint

2 tbsp chopped marjoram

A small bowl of mixed violet, primrose, nasturtium, rose, calendula, chive or gorse petals (it will depend on the time of year as to which petals you can pick)

1 sliced cucumber

3 hard-boiled eggs

2 peeled and sliced lemons

4 tbsp oil

2 tbsp vinegar

½ tsp salt

¼ tsp pepper

½ tsp sugar

Method

1. Wash the herbs and dry and break up roughly, cutting off any stems.

2. Mix the oil, vinegar, salt and sugar together

and toss the herbs in them.

3. Decorate with sliced peeled lemons, cucumbers and sliced hard-boiled eggs.

4. Sprinkle the flowers over the top and serve. NB. Do *not* pick petals from bulb flowers as they tend to be poisonous.

Beef Stew Without Fruit

I have to put this recipe in because it is so unusual for the period, even though it seems very ordinary to us today. Simply everything, if you could afford it, seemed to have the same dried fruit and spices in. While this recipe is untypical, it is still from the Elizabethan period.

1½ kg flank of beef joint

2 onions

3 large carrots

1 tsp salt

¼ tsp pepper

2 tbsp vinegar

125 g butter

Method

1. Stew the beef for 1 hour in water, then take it out, reserving the stock.

2. Chop the meat up and add it to a saucepan with chopped onions, grated carrots, seasoning, butter, vinegar and enough of the stock to cover it.

3. Simmer for another hour, and then boil vigorously for 10 minutes to evaporate the stock.

4. Serve on a dish of cubed bread.

Mutton Leg with Lemons

This is a sweet and sour lamb stew like the Baghdad recipe. I love the idea of putting it on top of bread cubes to soak up the juices. In this day and age we don't dip our bread into the gravy any more, but it really is very tasty if you do!

1 leg of mutton or 1 leg lamb

2 lemons

75 g currants

½ tsp pepper

1 tsp salt

2 tbsp vinegar

2 tbsp sugar

1 tsp sanders or 1 tsp red food colouring

1 loaf of bread cubes, with crusts cut off

Method

1. Boil the leg of lamb in water for 1 hour

2. Take off the meat and cut it into pieces. Put it in a pot, saving the stock.

3. Add the sliced lemons, currants, seasoning and enough stock to cover the meat.

4. Simmer for at least 1 hour until tender.

5. Add the sugar and vinegar and lastly the food colouring.

6. On a serving dish, lay the bread cubes and pour the stew on top of it and serve.

Boiled Rabbit with Stuffing (*to Boyle a Cony with a Pudding in his Belly*)

This is an interesting dish, and well worth trying.

1 rabbit, skinned and cleaned

250 g breadcrumbs

225 g suet

150 g currants

A mixture of savoury, parsley, marjoram and spinach – about a bunch in all

¼ tsp cloves

¼ tsp mace

1 tsp sugar

1 tsp salt

2 tbsp cream

2 egg yolks

75 g chopped dates

300 g gooseberries (stewed with the juice of a lemon, 3 tbsp sugar, ½ tsp salt and 50 g butter until soft)

Four thick slices of white bread, cubed, with the crusts taken off

300 ml mutton stock (use lamb stock cubes)

Method

1. Mix all the above ingredients together (apart from the stock and rabbit) and form a good stuffing.

2. Stuff the rabbit with the stuffing and sew it up tightly with string and a darning needle.

3. Make enough stock to cover the rabbit when it is placed in a big pan.

4. Boil and then simmer for 20 minutes per 450 g of rabbit.

5. Stew the gooseberries with the other ingredients. Put it in a dish on top of the bread cubes.

6. Lay the rabbit on top of the gooseberries and serve at once.

Boiled Chicken with Orange Sauce

1 capon
½ tsp mace
2 tbsp sugar
3 oranges
150 ml white wine
2 egg yolks
Method

1. Boil the chicken in salted water for 20 minutes per 450 g weight of chicken.

2. Take 150 ml of the stock it has been boiled in and put it in a saucepan with the wine, mace, sugar and oranges (peeled and sliced).

3. Simmer for 20 minutes and add the egg yolks to thicken, stirring all the time.

4. Put the cooked chicken on a platter and cover with the sauce and decorate the platter with slices of orange. Keep the rest of the stock for soup.

Liver Pate (Pudding of Hogges Liuer)

450 g pig's liver
75 ml cream
6 egg yolks and the whites of 2 eggs
200 g breadcrumbs
50 g raisins
50 g dates
¼ tsp mace
1 tbsp sugar
1 pinch saffron
50 g suet
Method

1. Poach the liver until it is cooked.

2. Mince the liver finely and use a food processor or mortar and bind the other ingredients with it.

3. Put in a dish and bake in a moderate oven until set – this should take about 30 minutes.

4. Cover with melted butter and eat with hot toast.

Boiled Pigeon with Rice Cream

2 pigeons
600 ml mutton stock or 2 lamb stock cubes and water
A bunch of marjoram, chives and thyme, mixed
150 ml double cream
50 g rice
¼ tsp mace
1 tbsp sugar
Salt and pepper to taste
Juice of 1 lemon
Method

1. Stuff the pigeons with the herbs and sew up the cavity with string.

2. Boil the pigeons in the mutton/lamb stock until cooked – 20 minutes per 450 g should be enough.

3. Slowly cook the rice in the cream and flavour it with the sugar, mace and salt and pepper.

4. Pour the cooked creamed rice onto a platter and place the boiled pigeons on top.

5. Squeeze over the lemon juice and serve.

Spit Roast Stuffed Eels

This could be done on a barbeque in the summer.

1 eel
1 onion, finely chopped
1 tbsp parsley, finely chopped
1 tbsp thyme, finely chopped
1 tbsp rosemary, finely chopped
¼ tsp pepper
1 tsp salt
A pinch saffron
100 g breadcrumbs
50 g melted butter
Method

1. Combine all the stuffing ingredients together with the melted butter.

2. Stuff the eel and tie it tightly with string, or better still, sew it up with string and a darning needle.

3. Lay it on the top grill of a barbeque and cook, turning when brown, or bake in a tray in the oven.

NB. This makes an interesting change to burgers, but be careful of the bones.

Fried Whiting and Apple Sauce

450 g whiting
Flour for coating
75 g butter
3 tbsp oil
1 minced apple
1 minced onion
150 ml white wine
1 tbsp lemon juice
1 tsp salt
¼ tsp pepper
¼ tsp cloves
¼ tsp mace

Method

1. Wash the fish and coat them in flour. Fry in the butter and oil until crisp and set aside.

2. Add the minced apple and onion to the pan and fry them for 5 minutes.

3. Put the apple and onion into a saucepan with the other ingredients and simmer for 10 minutes.

4. Put this mixture on a platter and top with the crispy whiting and serve.

Syllabub

3 x 600 ml pots of fresh double cream
600 ml white wine
A glass of Madeira wine or sherry
350 g fine caster sugar
Flavourings: either rosemary sprig or lemon peel

Method

1. Mix the wines and cream together with the sugar and beat until it makes a froth.

2. Pour into serving glasses and let them stand all night.

3. The next day, the curd will be thick and firm above and the drink clear under it.

4. To flavour it, add either a sprig of rosemary or some lemon peel to the glasses before pouring in the foam. You can also decorate it with primrose flowers brushed with egg white and sprinkled with sugar.

Rice Pudding

125 g white rice
900 ml milk
300 ml double cream
2 egg yolks
125 g brown sugar
¼ teaspoon salt
¼ teaspoon white pepper
¼ teaspoon ground cloves
¼ teaspoon mace
50 g currants
50 g pitted minced dates
2 tbsp butter

Method

1. Mix the rice and milk in a large pan and bring to a gentle boil.

2. Cover the pan and reduce the heat and simmer for about 30 minutes or until the rice is soft.

3. Add the cream and bring it to a boil. Reduce the heat and simmer for 2 to 3 minutes and remove from the heat.

4. In a bowl, mix the remaining ingredients and blend well.

5. Add this mixture to the rice and stir well.

6. Cover and cook for 5 minutes over a low heat.

7. Serve warm or chilled with extra cream if wished.

Tart of Strawberries

The strawberries that we take for granted now were a very new thing in Elizabethan Britain. Until they came from the Americas, the only strawberries available were the tiny wild strawberries, like the ones that still grow today in the valley where I live in Cornwall.

450 g fresh strawberries
50 g sugar caster sugar
¼ tsp cinnamon
50 g butter
50 ml rosewater
2 egg whites
75 g icing sugar
Sweet pastry for the base of a dish
Method
1. Line the dish with the pastry and bake blind.
2. Lay the whole strawberries on top.
3. Cream the caster sugar, butter and cinnamon together.
4. Dot the strawberries with the cinnamon butter.
5. Beat the egg whites until stiff and fold in the icing sugar.
6. Pile the meringue mix on top and bake in a hot oven until the meringue is just light brown.
7. Serve with cream.

Cherry Pottage

Apparently Queen Elizabeth's favourite fruit was the cherry, so I am sure she would have had this dessert.

4 slices white bread
250 g butter
1 glass of claret
125 g sugar (depending on whether the cherries are sweet or sour)
Method
1. Melt the butter in a large pan and fry the bread until it is golden. Put it in a pie dish.
2. Stone the cherries and put them in the pan with the claret and sugar if needed.
3. Bring to the boil and simmer for 5 minutes.
4. Pour this onto the fried bread and let it soak overnight before eating cold with cream.

Fine Crisp Butter Cake

175 g soft butter
125 g sugar
1 egg yolk, beaten
325 g sifted flour

½ tsp ground cloves
¼ tsp mace
A pinch ground saffron
1 egg white
Method
1. Cream butter and sugar in a bowl until light and fluffy.
2. Add the egg yolk and beat until thoroughly blended.
3. In another bowl, mix the flour and spices.
4. Sift the dry ingredients into the butter and sugar mixture and combine using your hands.
5. Press the mixture into a square dish that has been buttered.
6. Brush the top lightly with egg white and sprinkle with caster sugar.
7. Bake in a moderate oven for 45 minutes or until the cake feels firm when pressed lightly in centre.
8. Cut into squares while the cake is hot and allow it to cool in the dish (you could always make patterns in the top of the dough before cooking to make it more decorative).

Spinach Tart

I am not sure if this tart should be sweet or savoury. The recipe does not say whether the apples used are eating or cooking apples, so you could make it both ways to create an interesting talking point at a dinner party buffet!

450 g spinach
4 apples (either eating for sweet or cooking for savoury)
3 egg yolks
2 tbsp sugar
1 tsp cinnamon
¼ tsp ginger
Pastry shell pre-cooked in a dish
Method
1. Cook the spinach and the grated apples until tender and strain and dry well.
2. Put the spinach in the bottom of the pastry shell.
3. Beat in the egg yolks, the spices and sugar and pour over the spinach and apple.

4. Bake in a moderate oven for 20 minutes to set the egg yolks.

ELIZABETHAN CHRISTMAS FEAST

Of all the festivals held in Tudor Britain, Christmas was by far the favourite. They did observe Advent, however, which was a time of fasting and restraint before Christmas. So when they started their Christmas festivities at midnight on Christmas Eve, they could un-notch their belts and really indulge themselves! Strangely enough, though, New Year's Eve and Twelfth Night were celebrated the most.

Christmas was a time to let your hair down and just enjoy yourself. The traditional feast for the wealthy on Christmas Day was a deco-rated boar's head festooned with bay leaves and rosemary. The general populace, whilst not being able to afford a whole head, would have a large joint of pork, with side dishes of pig's ears and trotters or brawn. Some very wealthy households served the new meat – turkey – on Christmas Day, but it was not at that time thought to be as splendid a spectacle as a whole boar's head brought in by two servants on a huge platter!

In Lady Fettiplace's home they hung deco-rations of holly, mistletoe and yew around the house. To add to the excitement, they had trails of gunpowder running through the rooms, blazing trails and banging at their terminals giving off puffs of smoke. Gunpowder was easily come by during those times – I sup-pose they did not think it was dangerous as their floors were made of stone. This makes our Christmas cracker amusements seem very tame by comparison. They were also known to throw water bombs at each other across the table and open pies that made the ladies shriek as live birds and frogs jumped and flew out of them! I imagine that trick would only have

worked once, as those not too keen on frogs jumping into their laps would have stood well back when big pies were cut into in the future.

In much the same way as we used to put coins into out Christmas puddings, the Elizabethans would put a dried bean into the Twelfth Night cake. This cake was then divided amongst the whole gathering at the beginning of the evening, and the one who found the bean would become King or Queen Bean for the night. He or she was then in charge of the evening's entertainment. Because of this, it was sometimes devised who should get the trophy in advance, so that the group could ensure a good time was had by all! It is not certain what kind of cake the Twelfth Night cake was, but in some learned circles they think it was a ginger cake. I think this is interesting, as in my own family we always had to have a ginger cake at Christmas, as well as a Christmas cake, even though a lot of the family did not like ginger. We just had to have one, as it would not have been Christmas without spreading brandy butter on thick juicy slices of ginger cake during Christmas week. Maybe this tradition has derived itself from that of the Elizabethan Twelfth Night cake.

I think it would be great to revive the Twelfth Night tradition, as it would be the perfect excuse to have a party on 6 January instead of feeling depressed about the end of Christmas. I suppose at the end of the night you could always get your guests to help you take your decorations down too!

Wassailing was another tradition that the highest and lowest in the land enjoyed. It was originally said to be a winter fertility ritual to pay homage to the fruit trees and to drink their health in the hope that they would provide a good crop the following year. Depending on which part of the country you lived in, the basis of the drink could be cider, ale or beer. One thing common to all recipes was that it was sweet, spiced and hot, so it would have warmed your hands as you wandered around the orchards toasting the various fruit trees a bountiful year ahead of them. The peasants even extended the festivities for another day, which was called Plough Monday. This was the first Monday after Twelfth Night, which marked the beginning of the agricultural year. There might have been some leftovers from the big house that were given to the farm workers for this particular agricultural festival. I am sure there would have been a lot of leftovers after the Twelfth Night feast, at least in most households.

To Bake Turkey

The odd thing about this recipe is that it is so plain and simple, having looked through endless recipes from the period. It seems they put cinnamon, mace and ginger into almost everything, accompanied by raisins, dates and sugar. So it is strange that this turkey recipe is so very basic. Maybe it was such a new food – and so expensive – that they did not want to mask its natural flavour with the usual spices and dried fruit.

1 turkey

Salt

Pepper

Lots of butter

Method

1. Cleave the turkey on the back and bruise all the bones (these are the exact words in the recipe, so make of it what you will!).

2. Season with pepper and salt and put into it a good amount of butter.

3. Bake for 5 hours (it must have been quite a size!). Bake for the usual 20 minutes per 450 g plus another 20 minutes.

As they did not have foil to keep it moist, I imagine that even with lots of butter, the breast meat was probably very dry. It would have been served with rich gravy, made from the meat juices and red wine.

Herb Stuffing for the Turkey

225 g breadcrumbs

125 g suet

1 tbsp each of marjoram, thyme, mint, rosemary and parsley

2 eggs

1 tsp salt

½ tsp pepper

Method

Mix all the ingredients together and stuff under the skin of the bird before roasting.

Turnips Stuffed with Apples

These are a really good accompaniment to the turkey with bread sauce and cranberry jelly, known then as barberry jelly.

2 turnips the size of a large cooking apple

250 g minced cooked apple

2 tbsp currants

3 egg yolks, hard-boiled

50 g breadcrumbs

½ tsp salt

½ tsp cinnamon

¼ tsp ginger

1 tbsp sugar

300 ml water

150 ml white wine

50 g butter

1 tbsp vinegar

125 g dates, chopped

Method

1. Peel the turnip and cut the sides flat so it will stand up on both ends. Cut in half lengthways.

2. With a sharp knife, cut out the centre of the turnip so you have two bowls that will sit flat on the dish and sprinkle with salt.

3. In a bowl, mix the apple, currants, egg yolks, breadcrumbs, salt, cinnamon, ginger and sugar.

4. Put the mixture into the turnip bowls.

5. In a large pan bring the water and wine to the boil and add the butter to the water and stir.

6. Reduce the heat and place the turnips carefully in the pan. Cover with a lid and simmer

Turnips stuffed with apples. This is well worth making at Christmas as it is really unusual and goes well with game

for 1 hour until the turnips are soft when tested with a knife.

7. Add the dates to the simmering liquid and cook for 5 minutes more until the dates have absorbed it.

8. Serve at once with the date sauce poured over them.

Spinach Fritters

450 g spinach leaves
125 g chopped, cooked chicken breast
250 g brown breadcrumbs
2 eggs
50 g chopped dates
25 g currants
1 tsp sugar
½ tsp cinnamon
¼ tsp ginger
1 tsp salt
¼ tsp pepper

Batter
150 ml ale
75 g flour
1 egg

Method
1. Cook spinach in a little water, drain and press out all the liquid.

2. Chop the spinach finely and add the other ingredients and mix well. If needed, add more egg or breadcrumbs to make a stiff dough.

3. Roll into balls, dip into flour and then dip into the batter made of ale, flour and the egg.

4. Melt some butter in a pan and fry the fritter balls until brown on all sides.

5. Serve on a platter – these are good hot or cold.

Stewed Potatoes

700 g waxy potatoes

500 g cooking apples

5 tbsp brown sugar

¼ tsp cinnamon

1 small piece of freshly grated ginger

200 g butter

80 ml white wine vinegar

The rind of 2 oranges

Method

1. Parboil your potatoes in their skins, then peel them when drained.

2. Cut them into thin slices and put to one side.

3. Slice the peeled apples and also set aside.

4. Mix the ginger, cinnamon, orange peel, sugar, vinegar and butter together.

5. Lay in the bottom of an ovenproof dish some apples, then dot with the spice and butter mixture. Follow this with some potatoes and dot them with butter.

6. Repeat this until the dish is full and you finish with a potato layer.

7. Bake in a hot oven for 20 minutes until browned on top.

Grand Mince Pie (savoury)

Until the Victorian period, when tin baking tins were mass produced, small pies would be made in ceramic dishes. If a big pie was needed for a feast or festival, then a hot water crust pastry was used. This pastry, once mixed and left to get cold, is easily made into a freestanding pie shape and is strong enough to hold its shape without a tin in the hot oven. This is an original Elizabethan mince pie recipe, and would have been served cold as part of a buffet.

450 g minced beef

600 g suet

350 g currants

The peel of 2 lemons

2 eating apples, grated

½ tsp nutmeg

½ tsp cloves

1 tsp cinnamon

225 g sugar

225 g chopped dates

2 oranges

1 tsp caraway seeds

(Hot water pastry recipe below)

Filling

1. In a large bowl, mix all the above ingredients, apart from the dates, oranges and caraway seeds.

2. When well mixed, put the moulded pastry into your hand and cover with very thinly sliced orange pieces.

3. Top this with chopped dates and sprinkle on the caraway seeds.

4. Put a pastry lid on, binding the edges, and bake in a moderate oven for at least 1 hour.

5. Serve as a savoury centrepiece on a Christmas buffet.

Hot Water Crust Pastry

450 g plain flour

1 tsp salt

200 g lard

225 ml water and milk, mixed in equal quantities

Method

1. Mix the flour and salt together in a bowl.

2. Heat the milk and water in a pan with the lard until it boils.

3. Pour into the flour and beat well until it is smooth.

4. Let it go cold and then shape into the base and sides of your pastry with your hands. Once filled, top with a lid and seal it.

Compound Festive Salad

This is a good festive winter salad to go with the mince pie.

125 g blanched almonds, chopped

225 g big raisins

225 g dried figs, chopped

25 g capers

50 g olives, chopped

125 g currants

1 sprig sage leaves

Grand mince pie (savoury). We have all heard that the mince pies we eat at Christmas used to be made with minced beef, but this recipe shows how easy it is to make. It is a sort of sweet and savoury snack and really tasty too. Make it into small pies though unless you have an awful lot of guests for dinner!

300 g spinach leaves
3 oranges, peeled with a knife and sliced
2 lemons, peeled with a knife and sliced
300 g outer leaves of cauliflower, with the ribs removed
50 g sliced pickled cucumber (sliced and soaked in equal quantities of vinegar and water overnight)
25 g sugar
2 tbsp vinegar
4 tbsp olive oil
1 tsp salt
Sugar to garnish
Method
1. Mix or arrange all the above ingredients, apart from the oranges, lemons, oil, vinegar, sugar and salt, on a large platter.
2. Lay alternate rings of oranges and lemons on the top.

3. Mix the oil, vinegar, sugar and salt together and sprinkle over the salad.
4. Serve with savoury mince pies.

Brawn

For the poor cottage owner, brawn would have been the centrepiece of his Christmas feast. This was made from all the edible parts of a pig's head, including the eyes and brain, which have been cooked and set in jelly. It was traditionally eaten with bread and mustard. Thomas Tusser describes a husbandman's Christmas dinner: 'Good bread and good drink, a good fire in the hall, brawn, pudding and sauce with a good mustard with all.' Brawn was also mentioned in the Medieval period as a festive dish. So here is a Brawn recipe for you to try for yourself:
1 pig's head, cut into halves
300 g salt

1 tbsp whole peppercorns

8 onions chopped

2 tbsp dried sage

Method

1. Rub the salt all over the pig's head and put it in a pan. Leave for 2–3 days.

2 Take the brains out and poach them in water for about 30 minutes (this would disintegrate in the water on longer cooking).

3. Wash all the pieces well with cold water and put in a large pan. Just cover them with water and add the peppercorns, simmering for 2–3 hours until the meat is coming off the bones.

3. Lift the pieces onto a tray and leave the liquor to cool.

4. Take all the meat off the bones and mince it with a fork, adding the sage, chopped onion and pepper and salt to taste (some liked to keep the eyes and brains as a centrepiece, but this is up to you. If you don't want to do this, just mince the eyes with the meat and the poached brain).

5. Remove the fat from the surface of the liquor and strain it through a thick cloth.

6. Replace 4 quarts of this liquor into the cleaned pan and add the meat, onion and sage.

7. Simmer for 15 minutes, stirring frequently.

8. Have ready about a dozen pie dishes and basins and pour the mixture into them, leaving it to go cold.

9. When it is turned out it is a lovely glossy jelly and tastes delicious with applesauce and bread. NB. As it is not possible to make this without using a whole pig's head, I suggest you invite a lot of friends over to share the brawn with you at Christmas.

Christmas Plum Pudding

This is an Elizabethan recipe from Lady Elinor Fettiplace. It is interesting that there is no sugar in this recipe, as the fruit provides the sweetness. The brandy hard sauce recipe is almost identical to the hard sauce we still have at Christmas today, apart from the fact that we use brandy or rum instead of sherry. If there was any pudding left over the next day, it would have been fried in slices in butter and served with the hard sauce.

12 eggs

1 kg breadcrumbs

1 kg suet

3 kg mixed dried fruit (currants, sultanas, raisins, candied peel and dates)

3 pinches saffron

300 ml stout

2 tbsp brandy

1 tsp mace

Method

1. Soak the fruit overnight in the stout and brandy.

2. Next day, in a large bowl mix in the suet, flour and spice to make a thick dough.

3. Wet and then flour a large pudding cloth and put the mixture onto it. Tie it well.

4. Drop the pudding into boiling water and simmer for at least 5 hours.

Hard Sauce

225 g butter

225 g sugar

Sherry to mix

Method

1. Beat the butter and sugar together until light and creamy.

2. Beat in as much sherry as you can without it separating – usually about a glass will do.

3. Serve with the plum pudding.

Ginger Cream Tart

This makes a delightful yellow creamy tart – great for any festive occasion.

300 ml cream

3 eggs

1 tsp ginger

50 g chopped candied ginger (the ginger you get in jars of syrup)

2 tbsp ginger syrup

A pinch of saffron

1 tbsp boiling water

Pastry case in a dish, pre-baked

Method

1. Pour the boiling water onto the saffron to let out its colour and leave for 1 hour.

2. Beat the eggs and add the cream, ginger, ginger pieces chopped, syrup and the strained saffron water.

3. Pour into the pastry case and bake in a moderate oven for 35 minutes or until set.

4. Decorate with slices of ginger and serve.

Marchpane

An Elizabethan Christmas would be nothing if it did not include marchpane. This is a relatively simple version of the recipe, as most contain very large quantities of ingredients. In the original recipes, you have to crush the almonds in a mortar in order to grind them with the sugar, so this version should be much easier.

450 g ground almonds

450 g icing sugar

1 bottle/150 ml rosewater

Method

1. Combine the almonds and half the sugar together and work it to make a stiff paste, using a few drops of the rosewater.

2. On an icing sugar sprinkled board, roll out the marchpane to cover a baking tray (already lined with rice paper or non stick greaseproof paper).

3. Pinch the edges to make a sort of pie edge.

4. Bake in a moderate oven for 10 minutes or until it is hard to touch.

5. Mix the rose water with the rest of the icing sugar to make a thick icing.

6. Take out the marchpane and spread the icing on top, returning it to the oven until it rises – this should take about 5–8 minutes.

7. Take it out and dot it with comfits (sweets) and strips of edible gold leaf.

NB. The finished marchpane should look like a frosted pane of glass covered in sweets.

Candied Suckets (*Elizabethan sweets*)

450 ml rosewater

375 g sugar

2 large carrots or parsnips scraped and sliced into ⅛ inch discs

2 small apples or pears peeled and cored cut into ⅛ inch slices

1 cup fresh primrose, rose or marigold petals

Method

1. In a large saucepan, mix the rosewater and sugar and bring it to the boil.

2. Add the vegetable/fruit slices or flowers and stir gently.

3. Return to the boil and reduce the heat to cook gently for 15 minutes.

4. As soon as the sugar begins to caramelise (it turns light brown), remove the pan from the heat.

5. Remove the vegetable/fruit slices or flower petals and set out on wax paper. Refrigerate for 10 minutes.

6. Peel the candies off the waxed paper and store in an airtight container. This recipe makes about two dozen candies.

Sugar Plates and Sugar Glasses

These would have been a must at any Christmas feast in a wealthy Elizabethan home. They are plates and glasses made of sugar and were used to put all the suckets and delicate sweets in on the table.

5 ml gelatine

2 tsp lemon juice

4 tbsp rosewater

1 egg white beaten lightly

900 g icing sugar

Method

1. Mix the rosewater, lemon juice and gelatine in a bowl and put it over a pan of hot water to dissolve.

2. Stir in the beaten egg white and gradually add all the icing sugar to make a stiff paste.

3. Knead this sugar paste well until very smooth.

4. Roll onto a board dusted with corn flour

and, when thin enough, press it into the desired bowls and glasses used as the moulds.

5. The trimming must be kept to make the stems of the glasses or to steady the bowls on the table.

6. A little icing can be used to stick the bases on after they become hard in their moulds, which takes about 2 hours.

NB. A sugar bowl with the suckets in would look really nice on a table, especially if the bowl was then decorated with edible gold leaf.

A Dish of Snow

This is a really unusual dessert, but very Christmassy, and it comes from an Elizabethan cook book called *A Proper Newe Booke of Cokerye*. It is an artificial bush covered in creamy meringue snow that you are supposed to dip into with wafers.

300 ml double cream

6 egg whites

150 g icing sugar

1tbsp rose water

Method

1. Beat the egg whites until stiff.

2. Beat the cream until thick with the rosewater and sugar.

3. Fold the egg whites into the cream gently.

4. Cut two apples in half and put them on a silver platter. Into the apples stick large bushy sprigs of rosemary until you have a sort of rosemary forest on the platter.

5. Cast your snow onto the rosemary and the remainder around it. Then stick some sweets in the snow to make it look pretty. A dish of wafers could be put to one side of the dish so it can be eaten at the end of the meal.

Twelfth Night Gingerbread

Don't forget to put your bean wrapped in foil in the mix, so you can find your King or Queen Bean for the night!

300 ml honey

1 tsp ginger

¼ tsp cloves

¼ tsp cinnamon

¼ tsp ground liquorice

450 g breadcrumbs

1 tbsp anise seeds

Method

1. Heat the honey in a bowl over hot water. When it is really liquid, add the spices and then the breadcrumbs and continue to heat for 15 minutes until the bread has absorbed all the honey and spice.

2. Add your foil wrapped bean.

3. Pour the mixture into a dish lined with greaseproof paper and spread it evenly. Sprinkle with the anise seeds.

4. Cut it into the correct number of squares for the number of people you are going to invite to your twelfth night party and put it in the fridge to set.

NB. This is very sweet, so I would make sure the pieces are not too big for your guests to eat in order to find the bean!

THE CIVIL WAR

At this time the country was split not just by politics but also by food. There were stark differences between the frugal Parliamentarians and the decadent Royalist homes. The poor of the land, however, ate more or less the same as they had always done – pottages of beans and vegetables with the occasional bit of meat in it. Some of these peasants liked the idea of being treated as equals to their lords of the manor, but many lost their security as their Royalist lords had their lands confiscated by Parliament.

The subject of the Civil War is more than enough to fill a book by itself, and as this book is primarily looking at the diet of the people a the time, I will offer only a brief background to the war itself.

King Charles I and his French Queen Henrietta Maria apparently lived an extravagant life, oblivious to the needs of their poorer subjects. The King was said to be under the influence of his wife, who had no love for either the Protestant religion or Parliament. In the first four years of his reign, he dissolved three Parliaments because he did not like what they said. This in turn outraged many of the Puritan nobles of the time. The King seems to have been impervious to this, and between 1629 and 1640 he ruled the country without any Parliament at all. His extravagant lifestyle – some say encouraged by his French Queen – needed more and more funds to support it. In order to get these funds, the King made a new ship tax that included all British cities and not just ports, as they had done previously. This alone caused some unrest.

After a failed attempt by Charles and his Archbishop to Anglicise the Scottish church, the ensuing riots forced him to recall Parliament. That same Parliament then passed a bill that made it impossible for Charles to dissolve it without their prior consent. By March 1641, the Queen and her children had fled to Holland where she proceeded to sell her jewels to fund an army to fight the Royalist cause. By August 1642, England had descended into Civil War. Charles was subsequently beheaded in 1649 and the country became a parliamentary democracy under the stewardship of Oliver Cromwell.

These great events probably did not affect the diet of the ordinary British labourer and his family very much at all. It was the Royalist gentry, who under Cromwell's rule lost most of their lands and wealth, who would have noticed the greatest differences at their tables. The Puritan followers of Cromwell voluntarily rejected any culinary decadence as Papist, although I imagine that in the back rooms of some seemingly Puritan households, spices and exotic fruits were still consumed in secret, as many became Puritans for political rather than religious reasons. The humble mince pie was outlawed as a Papist food and Cromwell even passed a law in Parliament that made it illegal to eat one on Christmas day!

After King Charles II's return to the throne, he revived the extravagant palace banquets of his predecessors. Then a new revolution took take place, and that was marked by the publication of 'Lady's Cook Books'. Some of their titles included *The Compleat Cook Book*, *The Accomplish'd Lady's Delight* and *The English Hus-wife*. The motivation to write and publish these cook books came from those privileged enough to dine at court. Their mission was to pass on the delicacies of the King's French chefs to their less fortunate noble friends. It is thanks to this trend that we have such a wealth of recipes from this period today.

In the 1640s, the plantation owners of Barbados turned their land over solely to the production of cane sugar, which, at the same time, fuelled the need for slaves to work that labour intensive crop. This new preponderance of sugar gave birth to the biscuit we know and love today. Each town would promote its own special cake or biscuit, such as Shrewsbury biscuits, Eccles and Halifax cakes. As sugar became more plentiful in Britain, it became possible for the first time to preserve fruits over the winter – a revolutionary concept at the time. So all types of preserves were suddenly very much in vogue. A few new foodstuffs were also imported during those times, such as allspice or Jamaican pepper, and sago from Malaya.

In the poorer homes, however, one-pot cooking was the most common method at the time. This was not what we would call one-pot cooking today though. The one pot was a huge iron cauldron, in which were submerged bags of vegetables and nets of savoury dumplings and joints of meat for boiling. Pots had their lids sealed with pastry to cook chickens in herbs with butter and spices. So in a way, this one pot was the equivalent of our modern cookers. The pot with the sealed lid was like our oven and the boiled meat, pudding and vegetables were like having lots of different saucepans on top of the stove. This method of cooking was very fuel efficient as, having cooked a good many meals over a wood fire myself, I know how much wood is used up in just a single day's cooking.

By the post-Civil War period in 1682, due to this constant fuel problem, the first pressure cooker or steam digester was invented by a French physicist called Denys Papin, who lived in London at the time. It was basically a saucepan with a lid that screwed on to prevent any steam escaping. As the water boiled in the pan, the pressure and temperature went up, making the food cook faster. To prevent the pan from exploding, he devised a safety valve to take off excess pressure. He thought that his invention would primarily help the poor, who could make tough, cheap meat tender enough to eat, and as a by-product, a nutritious meat jelly with which to feed infants and the infirm.

The new prosperity in the towns during the middle of the seventeenth century saw the dining room come into fashion, with purpose-built oval tables and matching chairs for the diners to sit on. Sideboards were also made to match the style of the tables, from which numerous servants could serve the food. These sideboards were also designed to contain the fine pottery and silverware that the gentry were buying at the time *en masse*. This was because, during the Civil War, their silverware was melted down to fund the Royalist cause. It was not replaced until the restoration of the monarchy, when Charles II compensated the Royalists for their loyalty. So the genteel dinner party for just a few friends took the place of the baronial hall banquets for the majority of the nobility. It was a much more intimate affair altogether, and because of this, dainty delicacies were invented to serve at their tables.

Plain English Pottage

I will begin the recipes of this period by starting with the basic, plain English pottage eaten by most people at the time.

1½ kg joint of beef or mutton

50 g dripping

125 g oatmeal

1 handful parsley, chopped

1 handful sorrel, chopped

1 sprig thyme, chopped

1 sprig marjoram, chopped

30 peppercorns

Water

Salt to taste

Method

1. Cut the meat into cubes and brown in the dripping in a pan. Then transfer it to a large pot.

2. Add all the other ingredients and cover with water.

3. Bring to the boil and simmer overnight (if you have a slow cooker, this would be ideal).

4. Serve with lots of crusty bread to soak up the juices.

Lady Howe's Pease Pottage

400 g yellow peas

1 tsp salt

250 g butter

1 tsp fresh marjoram,

1 tsp fresh parsley

1 tsp fresh savoury

1 onion stuffed with cloves

¼ tsp mace

1 tbsp capers

1 French style loaf

Method

1. Cook the peas in lots of water, along with the salt and the whole onion stuffed with cloves.

2. Strain them when they are cooked.

3. Add the butter, herbs, spice and capers.

4. Bring to the boil.

5. Cut the French bread into pieces and toast. Lay the pieces the bottom of a shallow dish.

6. Pour the pottage over the toast, putting the clove-stuffed onion in the middle of the dish.

Fried Beans and Onion Cakes

225 g broad beans (pre-soaked overnight)

2 onions, finely chopped

2 garlic cloves

2 tsp powder douce

1 tsp salt

¼ tsp pepper

Goose fat for frying

Method

1. Boil the beans in fresh water until they burst and are soft.

2. Drain and press out all the liquid.

3. Add the minced garlic, chopped onion, spice, salt and pepper and mix well to a thick paste.

4. Heat the goose fat in a pan and fry burger-sized pieces until brown on both sides.

5. Serve with goose, stuffing and gravy.

A Pottage with Cabbage

For the Broth

1 blade mace

1 tsp cloves

4 onions

A bunch of fresh herbs (thyme, bay, marjoram, parsley)

1½ kg joint of any meat (pork, lamb, beef)

For the Pottage

2 French loaves

50 g butter

1 onion

1 cabbage (pre-boiled and chopped roughly)

2 tbsp flour

Method

1. Make a good broth by adding all the broth ingredients to a large pot and bringing to the boil.

2. Simmer for at least 2 hours, or for 4 hours if you have a slow cooker. The broth should by then be rich and tasty.

3. Strain the broth and put the meat to one side for later.

4. Then melt the butter in a frying pan and add the onions. Cook until golden, but don't let it brown.

5. Add the chopped, cooked cabbage to the pan and cook with the onions for a further 10 minutes, stirring all the time.

Civil War fried beans and onion cakes. These go very well with game

6. Add the flour and cook for another minute.
7. Gradually add the broth to the onions and cabbage and return the pottage to the large pot.
8. Slice the meat and toast the French bread, cutting it into cubes.
9. Add the meat and French bread cubes to the broth and bring to the boil. Serve at once.
NB. This recipe is great reheated the next day too.

Burdock Roots Bake

This is an interesting recipe, as I have used the burdock leaves in prehistoric cooking and I know that the Japanese use the roots in stir fries today, but apart from the dandelion and burdock drink, I have not seen it in any historic savoury recipes before.

450 g burdock roots, peeled
75 g butter
2 tbsp vinegar
2 tbsp sugar
250 g breadcrumbs
25 g butter for topping

Method
1. After peeling, leave the roots to steep in water for 1 hour.
2. Chop the roots and cook them in lots of boiling water until tender. Drain and chop finely.
3. Put the roots with the butter and vinegar in a pan and cook for 10 minutes on a low heat.
4. Layer one third of the mixture in the bottom of a baking dish and sprinkle with breadcrumbs and sugar.
5. Continue layering and top with bread-crumbs. Dot with 25 g of butter and bake in a hot oven for 10 minutes.
6. Serve at once with a meat stew.

Herby Pie

1 green lettuce
500 g spinach leaves
A sprig of winter savoury
A sprig of marjoram
75 g butter
½ tsp nutmeg

1 tsp sugar

1 tsp salt

125 g clotted cream

75 ml sweet sherry

Pastry – enough for a pie dish

Method

1. Line the pie dish with the pastry.

2. Chop the lettuce, spinach and herbs and put them on the pastry.

3. Top with the herbs, butter, nutmeg, sugar and salt.

4. Put the pastry lid on and bake for 30 minutes in a hot oven.

5. Take the pie out of the oven and, when cooled, take off the pastry lid and put the clotted cream and sherry in the pie.

6. Put the lid back on and then put it in the oven for a further 5 minutes to melt the cream. Eat at once.

The Best Way to Bake Larks, Sparrows, Blackbirds and Woodcocks

In no way am I suggesting that you go and catch a few blackbirds from your bird tables and try this recipe! But it is an authentic recipe from this period and I thought you would like to see it. I can't imagine there is very much meat on a sparrow anyway! Blackbirds, sparrows, larks and woodcocks could be replaced with quail, guinea fowl and pigeon.

1 tsp pepper

1 tsp salt

1 tsp ginger

A bunch of mixed, fresh garden herbs

75 g butter

2 egg yolks

Hot water pastry (see page 94)

Method

1. Truss the birds and parboil them.

2. Then take them out of the pan and put them in the pastry case.

3. Chop the herbs and mix with the butter, seasoning and ginger

4. Spread this herb butter over the birds and put

the pastry lid on (remember to pack them in tightly or the pastry will sag).

5. Bake in moderate oven for 40 minutes.

6. Take the lid off and pour in the beaten egg yolks. Put the lid back on.

7. Leave the pie to go cold before eating.

NB. This recipe says nothing about boning the birds, so I imagine it would have been a very fiddly business, separating them from the cooked egg yolks.

Meaty Dumpling

350 g lean minced beef

300 g beef suet

300 g breadcrumbs

2 tsp dried sage

½ tsp thyme

½ tsp savoury herb

2 eggs

75 ml cream

¼ tsp ground cloves

¼ tsp nutmeg

¼ tsp mace

2 tsp salt

Large cabbage leaves, blanched

Linen cloth

Mustard to serve with

Method

1. Mix all the ingredients together and form into a round ball.

2. Put a damp linen cloth on a board and flour it. Then cover it with the blanched cabbage leaves.

3. Put the mixture on top of the cabbage leaves and cover it with another leaf. Tie tightly with the pudding cloth.

4. Plunge into boiling water and simmer for 2 hours.

5. Take it out of its cloth and put it on a platter. Cut into wedges and serve with mustard.

Mrs Whitehead's Stew of Rump Beef

1 large slice of rump steak

1 tsp salt

½ tsp pepper

½ tsp nutmeg

1 tbsp fresh thyme, chopped

2 tbsp fresh marjoram, chopped

125 g beef suet

300 ml ale

300 ml water

300 ml white wine vinegar

300 ml white wine

Flour and water paste to seal the pot with

Method

1. Rub the beef with salt.

2. Mix herbs and suet together and roll it up in the rump steak. Tie tightly with string.

3. Put it in a ceramic pot with the ale, water, wine and wine vinegar. This should be enough liquid to cover the meat.

4. Seal the lid of the pot with flour and water paste and put in a slow oven for at least 3 hours.

5. Serve in a dish surrounded by the juices and eat with lots of bread to dip in the sauce.

Mrs Lord's Hash Recipe

500 g cooked pork

2 anchovies

A bunch of mixed herbs (marjoram, thyme, chives and parsley)

½ tsp pepper

½ tsp nutmeg

30 ml wine

3 shallots, chopped

125 g butter

250 g mushrooms

250 g coarsely chopped breadcrumbs

1 tbsp chutney

Method

1. Chop the meat finely and mix with the chopped anchovies, chopped herbs, pepper, nutmeg, salt, wine and chopped shallots.

2. Put the butter in a large pan and cook the mixture until it is hot.

3. When hot, add the chopped mushrooms and heat through thoroughly.

4. Add the breadcrumbs and a tablespoon of chutney of any kind.

Lady Sheldon's Gravy for Pork

This is very good with the 'Mrs Lord's Pork Hash' recipe

2 kg belly pork

1 litre water

1 tsp salt

1 tsp pepper

2 onions, chopped

Method

1. Cut the pork up very finely and fry it slowly until the fat runs from it.

2. Turn the heat up and brown the meat.

3. Add the chopped onion, pepper and salt and put it into a pot.

4. Cover it with water and seal the lid with flour and water paste.

5. Heat in a very slow oven for at least 5 hours. This makes 600 ml of good gravy.

Herring Pye

500 g short crust pastry

3 herrings, filleted

250 g currants

250 g raisins

250 g finely sliced onions

50 g butter

Salt and pepper to taste

Method

1. Line a deep pie dish with the pastry.

2. Layer some onions at the bottom of the dish and sprinkle with half the currants and raisins.

3. Dot with butter and salt and pepper.

4. Lay the herring fillets on top.

5. Add the rest of the onions, currants, raisins and butter.

6. Put the pastry lid on and seal well.

7. Bake in a moderate oven for 40 minutes and serve with boiled cabbage.

Savoury Toasted Cheese Four Ways

These recipes come from the closet of Sir Kenhelm Digby and, though simple, are well worth trying. Make a selection and serve at a party, with a variety of cheese fondue dips.

Bacon Toasted Cheese

250 g good mature cheddar cheese

50 g melted butter

300 ml milk

Salt and pepper

250 g chopped, fried bacon

White loaf, thickly sliced and toasted

Method

1. Into a pan, put the butter, milk and cheese and heat slowly until melted.

2. Chop and fry the bacon until crisp.

3. Pour the cheese sauce in a bowl and add the bacon.

4. Eat by dipping the toasted bread into the cheese mixture and scooping out the chopped bacon at the same time.

Onion and Cheese with Toast

250 g good mature cheddar cheese

50 g melted butter

300 ml milk

250 g finely chopped onion

Salt and pepper

White loaf, thickly sliced and toasted

Method

1. Simmer the onion in the milk until tender.

2. Add the butter, cheese salt and pepper.

3. Pour into a bowl and eat with the toast.

Scallops Toasted Cheese

250 g good mature cheddar cheese

50 g melted butter

300 ml milk

250 g scallops with coral removed

Salt and pepper

White loaf, thickly sliced and toasted

Method

1. Lightly cook the scallops in a pan with the butter and then chop them finely.

2. Add the cheese and milk and simmer.

3. Serve immediately with the toasted bread.

Asparagus Toasted Cheese

250 g good mature cheddar cheese

50 g melted butter

300 ml milk

Onion and cheese with toast. This is so simple, but you can't beat it for a supper snack

250 g peeled and chopped fresh asparagus
Salt and pepper
White loaf, thickly sliced and toasted
Method
1. Cook the asparagus in the milk until tender.
2. Add the cheese, butter and salt and pepper.
3. Serve in a bowl with the toasted bread.

Plaice in Garlic and Mustard Sauce

2 plaice fillets
1 tbsp chopped fresh thyme
½ tsp nutmeg
28 g butter
1 tsp English mustard
6 anchovy fillets
250 g butter
2 garlic cloves, crushed
2 tbsp wine vinegar
Salt to taste
Method
1. Score the skin of the fillets and rub in the chopped thyme and nutmeg and a little salt.
2. Put them skin side down in a greased pan and cook until the skin is brown.
3. Turn and brown the other side, then add the butter to the pan with the chopped anchovies, garlic, mustard and the vinegar and bring to the boil.
4. Serve at once with the garlic butter sauce.

Pigeon and Steak Stew

2 pigeons (whole, oven ready)
500 g braising steak
2 onions
2 sticks celery
2 carrots
1 tsp fresh thyme
1 tsp fresh oregano
1 tsp fresh sage
Salt and pepper
125 g butter
2 tbsp flour
1 glass brandy
2 tbsp redcurrant jelly

Method
1. Fry the onions in the butter until brown and put in the pot.
2. Brown the pigeons and beef in batches and put on top of the onions.
3. Add the flour to the pan juices and cook for 1 minute.
4. Add a cup of water to clean the pan and add this, along with the vegetables, salt and pepper, to the pot.
5. Cook in a slow oven for 2 hours or, if you have one, a slow cooker for 4 hours.
6. Just before serving, add a glass of brandy and the redcurrant jelly.

Cider Syllabub

300 ml cider
50 g caster sugar
A pinch of nutmeg
300 ml double cream
A little grated lemon zest
Method
1. Put the cider, sugar and cream in a large bowl.
2. Beat until thick and add the lemon zest.
3. Pour into serving glasses and sprinkle with nutmeg.
4. Leave in the fridge for at least 2 hours to set, and then serve.

Redcurrant Fool

300 ml cold custard
350 g redcurrants
3 tbsp sugar
150 ml double cream
150 ml water
Method
1. Cook the currants, sugar and water in a pan until tender.
2. Strain the currant puree and mix, when cold, with the custard.
3. Whip the cream and fold into the custard mixture.
4. Put into serving dishes and leave in the fridge

to set for 2 hours.

5. Garnish with redcurrants and serve.

Gingerbread

450 g plain flour
225 g dark brown sugar
150 g lard
300 ml sour milk
2 tsp ground ginger
Salt to taste
1 tsp bicarbonate of soda
300 ml black treacle
1 tbsp boiling water
Method
1. Cream the lard and sugar together and add the treacle and sour cream.
2. Add the bicarbonate of soda mixed with the boiling water.
3. Sift together the ginger, salt and flour.
4. Beat all the ingredients together.
5. Line a flat oblong dish with greaseproof paper and pour the cake mix into it.
6. Bake in a moderate oven for 40 minutes until set.

Diet Bread

This bread was made to help digestion.
400 g strong white flour
2 tbsp dried sage
20 g fennel seeds, bruised
15 g dried yeast
300 ml warm water
1 tsp sugar
Method
1. Mix all the dry ingredients with the warm water and knead as you would bread.
2. Leave in a bowl in a warm place for 1 hour.
3. Knock back and cut into 12 pieces and shape into twists. Leave to prove again on a tray in a warm place.
4. When doubled in size, bake in a hot oven for 35 minutes.

Knot Biscuits

3 egg yolks
1 egg white
125 g sugar
75 g butter
½ tsp mace
1 tsp caraway seeds
Pinch salt
300 g flour
2 tbsp rose water
Method
1. Beat the butter and sugar together.
2. Add the eggs and rosewater.
3. Mix in the rest of the ingredients together to make a thick paste. If it is too soft, add more flour.
4. Shape into knots or rings and bake as you would biscuits on trays in a hot oven for 10 minutes.

Trencher Bread

This is the typical bread of the day – it is very rich and nourishing.
300 g strong white bread flour
6 eggs
2 packets dried yeast
250 g butter
900 ml warm milk
1 tbsp salt
Method
1. Mix the dried yeast with the flour and the add salt.
2. Beat the eggs together with the warm milk.
3. Mix all the ingredients together and knead until springy.
4. Put in a warm place for 1 hour and knock back.
5. Put into three greased oblong dishes and bake for 35–40 minutes.

Lemon Cream

There are so many recipes from this period for lemon cream that it has to be included in this section. Here is a nice simple version:
2 x 600 ml pots of double cream

Knot biscuits. I love the caraways in seedy cake, if you do too you will like these dainty biscuits

Rind and juice of 2 lemons

6 egg yolks

200 g sugar (or more if you like it sweeter)

Method

1. Bring the cream slowly to the boil and add the finely grated lemon peel.

2. Take it off the heat and beat in the egg yolks and sugar.

3. Return to the heat and bring it back to the boil. Then simmer on a low heat, stirring all the time.

4. When it coats the back of the spoon, take it off the heat and keep stirring until almost cold (the easiest way is to keep putting the cream into cold bowls).

5. When cool, add the lemon juice and put into a serving bowl.

NB. The recipe states that you should keep stirring it every so often until really cold so that it will not form a skin.

CIVIL WAR CHRISTMAS

Leeches Christmas Broth

2 kg joint of beef

Ale – enough to cover it

450 g currants

450 g raisins

Half a white loaf, grated into breadcrumbs

1 tsp cloves, whole

2 tsp nutmeg

250 g prunes

1 glass red wine

Method

1. Put the beef and enough ale to cover it in a large pan and bring to the boil.

2. Simmer for 1 hour or until the meat looks tender.

3. Add the currants and raisins and bring back to the boil, stirring all the time.

4. After the fruit has swollen, add the grated breadcrumbs to thicken it.

5. Add the spices and simmer for 15 minutes. Then add the glass of wine.

6. The beef joint can then be sliced and put into bowls with the thickened broth to serve.

Christmas Turkey Two Ways: Boiled Turkey (to eat hot)

500 g sausage meat

2 tsp thyme

1 large turkey

1 handful of oatmeal

600 ml milk

600 ml water

250 g streaky bacon

12 large oysters

2 egg yolks

300 ml white wine

2 anchovy fillets

1 tsp nutmeg

450 g butter

2 lemons, cut into slices

Large muslin cloth

Method

1. Stuff the turkey neck with half the sausage meat and half the thyme.

2. Make balls with the rest of the sausage meat, roll them in streaky bacon and put to one side.

3. Tie the turkey up in the muslin cloth.

4. Bring the milk and water and oatmeal to the boil and put the turkey in it, simmering for 20 minutes per 500 g until cooked.

5. Take the turkey out of the liquid and the cloth and put it in a dish.

6. Fry the bacon and sausage meat balls and put in the turkey dish.

7. Dip 6 of the oysters in the beaten egg yolks and fry in butter. Put on the dish when browned.

8. Place the rest of the oysters in a pan with 1 tbsp butter and let them cook in their own liquor.

9. Make a sauce of the oyster liquor with white wine, anchovies and nutmeg and melt in some more butter.

10. Put all the sauce and oysters in the dish with the turkey. Bake in an oven to crisp the turkey skin and reduce the sauce – this should take about 20 minutes.

11. Serve with slices of lemon.

Bread Sauce for Turkey

1 onion

½ tsp salt

¼ tsp pepper

75 g white breadcrumbs

25 g butter

300 ml water

Method

1. Chop the onion and boil in the water with salt until cooked.

2. Add the butter, breadcrumbs, pepper and heat through before serving.

Christmas Turkey Two Ways: Boiled Turkey (to serve cold)

1 large turkey

250 g streaky bacon slices

2 tsp salt

1 tsp pepper

½ tsp mace

1 tsp nutmeg

¼ tsp cloves

3 bay leaves

1 tbsp chopped rosemary

600 ml white wine

1 litre water

2 tbsp mustard

50 g Demerara sugar

Method

1. Mix the salt, pepper, nutmeg, ground cloves and mace together and spread it on a plate.

2. Roll the bacon into the spices and put to one side.

3. Stuff the inside of the turkey with the bay leaves, a sprig of rosemary and the spiced bacon.

4. Sew up the cavity of the turkey with string and tie tightly in a cloth that has been floured.

5. Put the turkey in a pot with the wine and water that has already been brought to the boil.

6. Simmer with the lid on for 20 minutes for every 500 g of turkey.

7. When cooked, take it out of its cloth and put in a dish.

8. Smear the skin with mustard and then Demerara sugar and put in a hot oven for 20 minutes to crisp. Leave the turkey to go cold before serving.

Roast and Stewed Duck

1 duck

600 ml claret

2 onions

A bunch of mixed herbs (thyme, marjoram, parsley, garlic, chives)

25 g whole peppercorns

Method

1. Roast the duck for half the required cooking time.

2. Then put it in a casserole dish with the claret, onions, herbs and peppercorns.

3. Seal the casserole lid with flour and water dough for a perfect seal.

4. Cook for the remaining time in a slow oven.

5. Put the duck on a dish and reduce the gravy, which can then be served with the meat.

Baked Carrot Pudding

This is a good accompaniment for the roast and stewed duck.

400 g white breadcrumbs

400 g carrots, grated

8 egg yolks

3 egg whites

125 g butter, melted

1 small glass sherry

1 tsp nutmeg

600 ml milk

Method

1. Mix the breadcrumbs and grated carrot together.

2. Beat the eggs and add to the mixture.

3. Stir in the melted butter, a tablespoon of the sherry and the nutmeg.

4. Add milk to make a good thickness.

5. Bake it in a shallow dish in a hot oven for 30 minutes.

6. Just before serving, pour a little melted butter mixed with sherry over the top.

Christmas Mustard Pickle

1.35 kg of mixed vegetables (marrow, runner beans, onions, cauliflower, cucumber, cabbage)

100 g sugar

600 ml white vinegar

1 tsp turmeric

1 tbsp dry mustard

1 tbsp ground ginger

1 tbsp corn flour

Salt

Method

1. Prepare the vegetables by cutting them into the same sized pieces (generally the size of a hazelnut) and sprinkle with salt. Leave overnight.

2. Rinse and dry and put to one side.

3. Put the spices, vinegar and sugar in a pan and heat gently until the sugar has dissolved.

4. Add the vegetables and simmer for 15 minutes until tender. Blend the corn flour with a spoonful of the vinegar and the dry mustard and add it to the pan.

5. Bring it back to the heat and boil for a few minutes until thickened.

6. Put in pots and seal until used.

Lady Howe's Little Plum Puddings

This is an interesting take on the traditional Christmas pudding.

2 eggs

125 g dark brown sugar

2 tbsp rose water

1 tsp vinegar

300 g currants

1 tsp nutmeg

125 g beef suet

Pinch of salt

200 g breadcrumbs (or just enough to make stiff dough)

Butter muslin, cut into squares

Method

1. Beat the eggs well with the butter, rosewater and vinegar.

2. Add the currants, nutmeg and beef suet.

3. Add the salt and enough of the breadcrumbs to make stiff dough.

4. Individually wrap the balls in floured butter muslin cloths.

5. Drop the balls into a pot of boiling water and simmer for 35 minutes until firm to the touch.

6. Take them out of the muslin. Serve on a plate, piled high and covered with melted butter, sugar and rosewater.

Christmas Pudding: Aunt Franckline's Recipe

Breadcrumbs from a small white loaf, with crusts taken off

300 ml whole milk

300 ml double cream

1 tsp nutmeg

4 eggs

125 g flour

125 g beef suet

350 g mixed currants and raisins

Pinch of salt

Muslin cloth

Method

1. Bring the milk and cream to the boil and pour over the breadcrumbs. Mix well.

2. Leave to stand for 2 hours.

3. Add nutmeg and beaten eggs and mix it all together well.

4. Add the flour a handful at a time as you mix it.

5. Stir in the suet, currants, raisins and salt and tie it in the muslin cloth.

6. Drop into boiling water and simmer for 3 hours.

Sack or Sherry Cream

This makes a nice alternative to brandy butter with your pudding from Rebecca Price.

8 tbsp thick cream

4 tbsp sherry

2 tbsp sugar

1 tbsp orange zest

Method

1. Beat the above ingredients together and serve at once with your pudding.

Aunty Rye's Long Biscuit Cream Recipe

Though it has no fruit or jelly in it, I think this pudding is the forerunner of the sherry trifle. A Christmas must have, I think!

1 packet of boudoir sponge fingers

500 ml double cream

8 egg yolks

3 tbsp sweet sherry

125 g sugar

2 tbsp rose water

1 blade of mace

Method

1. Break the biscuit fingers into pieces and put in a dish.

2. Bring the cream to the boil with the mace and remove the mace once boiling.

3. Add the beaten egg yolks and cook slowly, stirring all the time until it begins to thicken.

4. Add the sherry, rosewater and sugar to the sponge fingers and leave for 1 hour to allow it to be absorbed.

5. Pour the custard over the sponge fingers and serve with fruit when cold.

Newton's Chocolate Cream

It would not be Christmas without chocolate, and during this time it was still a great extravagance and only for the rich. If you are watching your weight, only make a small quantity because it is so delicious!

500 ml double cream

75 g good dark chocolate, grated

3 egg yolks beaten into 2 tbsp of double cream

Newton's Chocolate Cream. If you like chocolate and custard you will love this combination, it did not last long after I took the picture of it!

150 g sugar (or more if you like it sweeter)
Topping
150 ml double cream
1 egg white
25 g chocolate, melted
25 g sugar
Method
1. Bring the cream to the boil and then take it off the heat.
2. Stir in the chocolate and keep stirring all the time until it is melted.
3. If the cream cools too soon, put it back on a gentle heat until the chocolate is melted.
4. Add the egg yolks, pre-mixed with the cream, and return to a gentle heat, stirring all the time.
5. When it coats the back of the spoon, take it off the heat and stir in the sugar.
6. Take two large bowls and pour the mixture into one of them. Then hold the full bowl high in the air and pour the mixture into the other bowl, repeating this action at least ten times.

This should form a nice froth in the mixture. Then let it set until it is cold.
7. To make the topping just before serving, whip the cream and add the melted chocolate.
8. Whip the egg white until stiff and fold into the cream and chocolate with the sugar.
9. Pour on top of the chocolate creams before serving.

Christmas Cake

Christmas cake seems to have been huge in the most genteel of households in the seventeenth century. In Rebbeca Price's family cookbook of the period, she had over seven Christmas cake recipes. Most involve starting with 4 kg of flour and over 24 eggs! Here is Rebecca's list of ingredients for what she describes as 'a very good and rich cake, often made by me'.

4 kg flour
500 g sugar
3 nutmegs
1 tbsp each of cinnamon, mace and cloves
4 grains of musk
1 kg ground almonds
20 eggs
4 egg whites
1 quart of good fresh yeast water
1 quart double cream
1 kg butter
150 ml orange flower water
150 ml damask rose water
300 ml sherry
4½ kg currants
1 kg raisins
500 g dates
500 g candied orange peel
500 g candied lemon peel
1 kg other candied citron peel

Rebecca states that this will make a very large cake! What size dish or oven did she have, I wonder? At the end of the recipe, she says that if you want to make 'an extraordinary great cake', you may 'add one third part of everything on top'. In other words, start with 6 kg of flour and so on! Below is a recipe from the same book for a more modest cake, but interestingly enough, these cakes were not covered with marzipan and iced. They were iced with glace icing straight from the oven and put back in the oven briefly for the icing to harden.

Modest Christmas Cake Recipe

500 g plain flour

500 g sugar

500 g butter

6 egg yolks

500 g currants

1 glass sherry

2 tsp cinnamon

1 tsp nutmeg

250 g icing sugar

Method

1. Beat the egg yolks with the sugar until pale.

2. Pour the sherry into a bowl with the currants and set them near the fire to plump up.

3. Melt the butter and add to the eggs and sugar with the flour.

4. Add the plumped currants and bake in a moderate oven for 1½ hours or until firm to the touch.

5. Mix the icing sugar with a little water and spread over the hot cake.

6. Put the cake back in the oven for another 5 minutes until the icing is hard, but not brown.

Seventeenth-Century Christmas Brandy Punch

2 litres spring water

350 g white sugar

The juice of 12 lemons

1 litre brandy

1 tsp nutmeg, grated

Method

1. Mix the water and sugar together and heat slowly in a pan, stirring all the time until the sugar has dissolved.

2. Add the lemon juice, nutmeg and brandy and bring to a simmer.

3. Simmer for about 30 minutes until the nutmeg has flavoured the drink and serve while hot.

Spiced Wine (Hippocrass)

1 litre sherry

2 litres red wine

4 cinnamon sticks

1 bruised ginger root

1 nutmeg

1 tsp cloves

1 tsp coriander seeds

350 g sugar

1 sprig of fresh rosemary

2 lemons sliced

300 ml milk

Method

1. Into a pan, put the wine and the herbs and spices and bring to a simmer. Leave in a warm place overnight to infuse.

2. Strain in the morning and add the sugar, the sherry and the milk.

3. Strain through fine muslin to clear the wine and serve warm.

Stepony

This recipe does not say how long it should be stored, but if stored for three months or more it becomes quite alcoholic.

1 gallon of water

450 g raisins

225 g sugar

The rind and juice of 2 lemons

Method

1. Mix all the ingredients apart from the water together in a large container.

2. Boil the water and pour it over the other ingredients.

3. Stir it well and let it stand for 24 hours.

4. Strain and put it into bottles and store them in a cellar.

THE GEORGIANS

Think of the Royal Crescent and Jane Austen centre in Bath and we have arrived at the Georgian period, characterised by genteel dances at assembly rooms, where mothers sought good suitors for their daughters. But outside that cosseted genteel world were the stirrings of the Industrial Revolution, and new towns were being built to house vast work forces that left their rural idyll for the riches of the towns. While there was always a large gap between the nobility and the peasantry, it was somehow becoming more palpable as they were both living in the same towns. Beggars would sit on frosty street corners and watch gilt carriages sweep past carrying ladies wrapped in furs. This movement to the towns also had a much greater effect on the food of the poor than had been seen in any other period. In the country, the farm worker at least had access to wild berries and nuts and an endless supply of root vegetables. In the towns, however, the factory workers crammed into their tiny terraced houses had no room to grow anything with which to supplement their basic diet.

There were also serious transport problems during this time, as the raw materials needed to manufacture their goods were brought to the new towns via muddy and badly maintained roads. More importantly, though, the labour force for the new factories also needed their food brought to them, and so the first canals were built in the to solve this problem. They also made it possible to transport delicate goods from the factories to the coastal ports. Josiah Wedgwood built his pottery works alongside these canals in order to transport his china without breakages throughout the country and onto ships at various ports.

At the other end of the scale, chocolate and coffee houses became the centres of fashionable social life. There were at one time over 500 in London alone. There were also chocolate and coffee houses for the supporters of various political parties: The Coco Tree Chocolate House for the Tories, for instance, and St James Coffee House for the Whigs. Alcoholic drinks were not served in these houses, but pipe smoking was very common. Coffee houses, however, went into decline in the mid-eighteenth century, as tea drinking became the universal British pastime. It was drunk in even the poorest homes throughout the land by the reign of George III. Tea was always drunk black at first, as it was in the countries it came from, until someone suggested that it could damage the stomach if drunk too frequently. And so it was suggested by medical men at the time that if a little milk was added to the tea, it would line the stomach and the drink could be enjoyed as frequently as desired.

This was also a time of great innovations in the kitchens of the stately homes, with the invention of a newly-devised clockwork mechanism for turning the spit on which whole pigs or sheep were roasted. This device subsequently took the place of a poor kitchen worker, who would previously have spent all day manually turning those great spits whenever there was a great banquet planned. This period also saw the beginnings of the mass-produced oven. Until then, most people sent their pies to the local baker to have them cooked, as they had always done. But with the improved ironworks of the blossoming Industrial Revolution, ovens became more widely available.

The development of printing presses, too, introduced the middle classes to all manner of educational pursuits, of which cookbooks were one of the most popular. At first, the books were primarily the recipes of the famous French chefs of the time, who created gastronomic wonders for the aristocracy – dishes that the newly rich wanted to taste for themselves. But the war with France during the eighteenth century encouraged a new wave of patriotic cooking. Some of the well-known cookery writers of the day, such as Hanna Glasse, promoted good English cooking in her books. Her book, *The Art of Cookery Made Plain and Easy,* was said to have gone into at least 16 editions between 1747 and 1803.

Another fascinating development was the icehouse, many of which were being made in the country estates. I have been fascinated by these ever since I first heard about them, and have seen one or two in stately homes in Scotland. The idea was that great, underground, dome-roofed rooms were constructed and, when the lakes on the estate froze solid in the winter, the groundsmen would cut great chunks of ice from the lakes and stack it between layers of straw in the icehouses. Then, in the heat of the summer months, when the Lady of the manor required delicate ices, she would order that ice was brought up to the kitchens. The ice was then crushed and mixed with salt to form a slush that was packed into double-skinned bowls, into which cream and custards were poured. With a little hard whipping by the cook, the icy walls of the bowl would turn it into ice cream for the guests at the dinner table. The ice never came into direct contact with the food, so it was actually very hygienic. These ice creams were very often married with the exotic fruits grown in the hot houses of the estate – a delight for all those privileged enough to eat it.

One of the most enduring culinary inventions in the world was said to have been invented during this period also, and that is the humble sandwich! Legend has it that John Montagu, 4th Earl of Sandwich, instructed his chef to devise such a snack. He was a keen gambler and during a 24-hour card game marathon, he asked his chef to devise something for him to eat that required no fork or knife and that he could eat with one hand, while holding his cards with the other. The chef gave him a slice of meat between two pieces of toast, which fulfilled all the Earl's requirements. This then became a popular snack in gambling circles and is now the world's most popular snack, eaten most frequently by people on the move.

Asparagus Omelette

1 bundle of fresh asparagus
6 eggs
50 g butter
Salt and pepper to taste
Parsley to garnish
Method
1. Boil the asparagus in water until it is tender.
2. Beat the eggs.
3. Melt the butter in the pan and add the eggs and the chopped, cooked asparagus.
4. Sprinkle the salt and pepper over it and cook until set.
5. Put on a plate and garnish with parsley before serving.

Potted Beef

All types of meat were potted at this time, not only to preserve them, but also so that dainty sandwiches could be made ready for teatime in wealthy ladies' parlours.

1 kg beef
100 g butter
4 tbsp flour
½ tsp salt
1 tsp ground cloves
2 tsp nutmeg
1 tin anchovy fillets
¼ tsp pepper

Method

1. Put the beef in a tight fitting dish with a lid.
2. Slice half the butter and put it on top of the meat.
3. Seal the dish with flour and water paste.
4. Bake in a slow oven for 3 hours or in a slow cooker (if you have one) for 4 hours.
5. Take the meat out and mince it in a food processor or hand mincer.
6. Add all the other ingredients, plus the fat from the stock in the pot, and mix well.
7. Press the mixture into small pots and cover with the rest of the butter, melted to seal the meat.

Oysters in Bread Rolls

4 dinner rolls
75 g butter
30 ml white wine
12 fresh oysters
2 tbsp finely chopped parsley

Method

1. Cut the tops off the rolls and scoop out the contents.
2. Brush the insides with melted butter.
3. Put the rolls in the oven until crisp.
4. Fry the oysters in the rest of the butter until cooked.
5. Add the wine and parsley to the pan and divide into the hot rolls, replacing the lid.

Battered Celery Hearts

I am not usually that keen on cooked celery, but this recipe is really tasty.

5 or 6 small celery hearts
200 g flour
¼ tsp nutmeg
A small glass of wine
2 egg yolks
1 tsp salt
50 g butter

Method

1. Make the batter with the egg yolks, flour, nutmeg and wine.
2. Cut the celery hearts in half and boil in water until they are almost cooked.
3. Drain well and pat dry.
4. Dip each piece in the batter and shallow fry on all sides in butter.
5. When cooked, pour melted butter over the battered hearts and serve.

Beetroot Pancakes

200 g peeled, cooked beetroot (you can buy packets in the supermarket, but check it has no vinegar on it)
40 ml brandy
4 tbsp double cream
4 egg yolks
150 g flour
2 tbsp sugar
Butter
½ tsp nutmeg

Method

1. Mash the beetroot well (if you have a ricer, all the better).
2. Mix with all the other ingredients, apart from the butter.
3. Melt the butter in a shallow pan, and when it is hot, drop spoonfuls of the mixture into it (about the size of a small, round cracker).
4. Turn when they start to bubble. These are equally good hot or cold, and very good with Horseradish sauce.

English Rarebit

2 thick slices of brown bread

Small glass of red wine

225 g cheddar cheese

Method

1. Toast the bread.

2. Put it in a shallow dish and pour over the red wine.

3. Slice the cheese and place it in a thick layer over the bread.

4. Put it in the oven until the cheese has melted and gone golden brown.

Ragoo of Pigs' Ears

4 pig ears

2 glasses of wine

2 glasses of water

1 tbsp flour

50 g butter

1 anchovy, finely chopped

4 shallots, finely chopped

1 tsp English mustard

Salt to taste

The juice of 1 lemon

Method

1. Boil the ears in the water and wine until tender.

2. Drain, saving the stock, and cut the ears into slices.

3. Sprinkle the flour in the stock and bring to the boil to thicken.

4. Fry the pork slices in the butter until brown.

5. Add the stock and the rest of the ingredients to the pan and simmer.

6. Serve at once with fresh bread.

Beef Stew

2 rump steaks

Salt and pepper to taste

300 ml water

1 blade of mace

3 cloves

A bundle of sweet herbs (parsley, thyme, savoury, marjoram)

1 anchovy fillet

50 g butter

50 g flour

150 ml white wine

1 onion, quartered

10 oysters

Flour for dusting

50 g butter for frying

Method

1. In a pan, lay the steaks and cover with the rest of the ingredients (apart from the oysters, flour for dusting and the butter for frying).

2. Cover and stew until the steaks are tender.

3. Take the steaks out of the pan, dust them with flour, and fry them in the butter until brown.

4. Strain the gravy and pour it into the pan. Toss the steaks in it until hot and thickened.

5. Add the oysters and cook for 5 minutes in gravy.

6. Pour into a dish and garnish with pickle.

Three ways to serve Fried Sausages: Dish 1

225 g sausages

6 apples

Method

1. Peel and core the apples. Slice four thickly and quarter the other two.

2. Fry the sausages in a pan with the sliced and quartered apples.

3. Serve the sausages in a dish with the apples all around them. Garnish with the apple quarters.

Three ways to serve Fried Sausages: Dish 2

225 g sausages

225 g cabbage, sliced and boiled

Method

1. Fry the sausages in a pan and put to one side, keeping them warm.

2. Fry the cabbage in the sausage fat until it is browning on the bottom. Stir well and put into a dish topped with the sausages.

Ragoo of pigs' ears. If you like pork crackling you will probably like this. The mustardy onions it is served with are definitely an acquired taste though!

Sausages and Pease Pudding. This is a great mid-winter dinner. We just don't eat enough mushy peas anymore!

Three ways to serve Fried Sausages: Dish 3

225 g sausages

400 g cold Pease pudding (made with dried peas, stock and onions)

Method

1. Fry the sausages and keep warm.

2. Fry the Pease pudding in the sausage fat until it browns. Stir well and put into a dish.

3. Stick the sausages into the Pease pudding and serve.

Breaded Ham

1 large ham

2 beaten eggs

150 g breadcrumbs

73 g melted butter

Method

1. Soak the ham overnight in water if it is smoked and then change the water.

2. Boil the ham for the time required on the packet.

3. Take the ham out and pull off the skin. Coat it with the egg and then the breadcrumbs, and pour the melted butter evenly over it.

4. Bake for a further 30 minutes in the oven.

NB. It is interesting to note that breaded ham recipes have not changed much since the Georgian period.

Salmagundi

This dish would be a main meal salad today, but in the Georgian period it was a side dish or middle dish for supper.

The meat from 2 roast chickens, minced well

6 hard-boiled eggs (yolks and whites minced separately)

3 lemons, peeled and sliced finely

1 tin of anchovies

A bunch sorrel leaves

300 g spinach

4 sliced shallots

2 oranges, sliced thinly

1 tbsp horseradish, grated (you can use the horseradish in a jar, but not the creamed variety)

3 tbsp oil

Juice of 1 lemon

1 tsp mustard

Salt to taste

Method

1. On a large platter, spread a layer of the minced chicken.

2. Then place over the chicken a layer of minced egg yolks, a layer of anchovies, and a layer of minced egg whites.

3. Put the slices of lemon on top, and then a layer of sorrel and spinach (uncooked).

4. Top the spinach with the sliced shallots and finally with the sliced oranges.

5. Make the dressing by mixing the oil and lemon juice with the mustard and salt.

6. Pour this over the oranges and garnish with the horseradish.

7. The salmagundi can then be sliced from the top in wedges and served on small plates.

Cheshire Pork Pie

This is an interesting pork pie with an apple layer inside it.

450 g loin of pork

½ tsp salt

¼ tsp nutmeg

¼ tsp pepper

4 eating apples, peeled, cored and sliced

1 tsp sugar

300 ml white wine

75 g butter

2 pig trotters for jelly

Hot water pastry (see below)

Method

1. With the pastry, mould the base and sides of your pie using your hands.

2. Cut the pork into steaks and rub with the spice and seasoning.

3. Lay half the pork loin on the bottom of the pie dish.

4. Put in a layer of sliced apples and sprinkle with sugar.

5. Put the remaining pork on top of the apples.

6. Pour the wine on top and dot with the butter. Put on the pie lid, sealing it well with water.

7. Bake in a moderate oven for 1 hour on a baking tray.

8. Put the trotters in a pan of water with some salt and boil well for 1 hour. Strain the stock and keep to one side.

9. When the pie is taken out of the oven, carefully make a hole in the lid and fill it with as much of the trotter stock as you can. Leave to cool (this stock will form the jelly traditionally seen in any pork pie). Serve cold.

Hot Water Crust Pastry

This is your classic pork pie pastry.

450 g plain flour

1 tsp salt

200 g lard

225 ml water and milk mixed in equal quantities

Method

1. Mix the flour and salt together in a bowl.

2. Heat the milk and water in a pan with the lard until it boils.

3. Pour into the flour and beat well until smooth.

4. Let it go cold and then shape into the base and sides of your pie with your hands. Once filled, top with a lid and seal it.

A Fancy Dish of Herrings

12 small herrings

A large bunch of parsley

300 ml parsley sauce (made with whole milk, parsley, flour and butter)

100 g butter

50 g seasoned flour (just add salt and pepper to it)

Method

1. In a large pan, melt the butter and dust the herring with flour. Fry until crisp on both sides. Set to one side and keep warm until they are all cooked.

2. Make the parsley sauce.

3. Fry the parsley in the same pan as the fish until it is crisp, but has not lost its colour.

4. Place a small, upturned cup in the middle of a large platter and surround it with the fried parsley.

5. Place the fish around the platter with their heads on the rim and their tails sticking up over the cup. The cup should be quite small, so that it does not stop the tails meeting each other. It should lift them slightly to bend them up.

6. Serve with parsley sauce.

Salmon Pie

1 whole salmon

250 g gooseberries (frozen will do)

1 tsp allspice

¼ tsp black pepper

½ tsp nutmeg

1 tsp salt

500 g made puff pastry

225 g butter

25 g flour

Method

1. Fillet the salmon and cut the fish into nice thick slices.

2. Boil half the gooseberries in enough water to cover until soft and strain, retaining the liquor.

3. When the gooseberry liquor is cold, brush each piece of salmon with it and rub in the spices and salt.

4. Put the fish (apart from 4 slices) into the bottom of a pastry-lined dish and cover with a pastry lid. Bake in a moderate oven for 1 hour.

5. While the salmon pie is cooking, boil the fish bones in water for 1 hour until reduced by half.

6. Melt half the butter in the pan and fry the rest of the salmon until the pieces are golden brown.

7. Add the strained fish stock to the fish and bring it to the boil. Simmer until thick.

8. Take the pie out of the oven and cut off the pastry lid.

9. Strain the gravy and add to it the other half of the gooseberries and butter.

10. Bring back to the boil and simmer for 10 minutes until the gooseberries are soft.

11. Pour this gravy and the fried salmon over the salmon in the pie and replace the lid. Set it aside to go cold.

Apple Fritters

4 large Cox's orange pippin apples

1 glass of brandy

75 g sugar

1 tsp cinnamon

The peel of one lemon

50 g lard

3 tbsp flour

Method

1. Peel, pare and quarter the apples.

2. Put them in a dish with the brandy, sugar, lemon peel and the cinnamon.

3. Leave them overnight.

4. Take them out and dry them. Then dust them in flour and fry until golden in the lard.

5. Lay them in a dish covered with more sugar and serve with the brandy marinade in a jug.

Apple and Custard Pie

This is a wonderful recipe – apple pie and baked custard all in one!

500 g puff pastry

4 large cooking apples

225 g sugar (this depends on how sharp the apples are)

Lemon peel and juice

2 egg yolks

300 ml double cream

½ tsp nutmeg

1 blade of mace

Method

1. Line the sides of a dish with two thirds of the puff pastry.

2. Roll out the other third for the lid and put to one side.

3. Pare and quarter the apples and take out the cores.

4. Slice the apples and lay them in a thick row on the pastry.

5. Sprinkle over half the sugar.

6. Sprinkle with lemon peel and lemon juice.

7. Boil the peelings and core with the mace in a little water until they are soft and strain.

8. Pour this onto the apples and put on the pastry lid. Bake for 35 minutes in a hot oven.

9. Take the lid off the pie and put it carefully to one side, leaving the pie to cool.

10. Beat the egg yolks in the cream with the rest of the sugar.

11. Pour this custard on top of the apples in the pie and sprinkle with nutmeg.

12. Put the lid back on the pie and bake in a cool oven for 40 minutes until the custard is set.

13. Let the pie go cold before serving.

Fairy Butter

These were kept chilled until ready for use and eaten with wafers or plain cakes like a rich butter cream.

4 hard-boiled egg yolks

2 tbsp rose water

50 g sugar

150 g unsalted butter

Method

1. Mash the egg yolks and mix with the other ingredients.

2. Press through a fine metal sieve until you have little ringlets of the butter.

Seedy Shortcake

These were very popular in Georgian times. Caraway seeds were used to help digestion, and this is still a proven remedy today.

225 g butter

225 g flour

1 egg

150 g sugar

1 tbsp caraway seeds

50 g raspberry jam

Method

1. Beat the butter until it is pale and soft. Add the sugar and then the egg.

Apple custard pie. I loved this; it was like eating apple pie with crème brûlée inside. Delicious!

2. Beat in the flour and caraway seeds.

3. Roll onto a floured board and use a wineglass as a cutter.

4. Place on a baking tray and prick them all over. Bake in a hot oven for 10 minutes until they turn a pale golden colour.

5. Serve hot, spread with raspberry jam.

Pistachio Cream

This makes a lovely green custard pudding. For a good effect, it can be served with bright red jelly!

225 g pistachio nuts

300 ml cream

2 egg yolks

50 g sugar

50 g pistachio nuts, sliced lengthways for decoration

Method

1. Shell the nuts and chop them. Put them, along with the cream, into a pan with the egg

yolks and sugar mixed well together.

2. Stir over a gentle heat until thick, but do not let it boil.

3. Put it into a soup plate and let it go cold.

4. Decorate with the sliced nuts or surround it with red jelly. Serve immediately.

Sherry Trifle

This is another step closer to our present-day version of the sherry trifle, in that there are three separate layers. It is definitely an adult dish, though, as there is a lot of wine and sherry in it!

225 g ratafia biscuits

1 glass sherry

300 ml cold custard

300 ml syllabub (made by beating double cream, sugar and wine together with lemon zest – see the Civil War recipe for cider syllabub, but use wine instead of cider)

To garnish: flowers, crystallized fruits such as angelica and cherries

Smoked fish stew is so quick and easy to make and is always delicious

Nutty scrambled eggs could be an interesting Christmas breakfast dish, Roman style

Dates Alexandrine is simple to make, but very impressive as an after dinner treat

Roman Christmas feast. Why not give turkey a miss this year and go Roman Christmas style!

This Medieval cabbage stew with cardamom and fennel seeds in the powder douce makes this vegetable stew something really different to serve with roast meats or fish

Syllabub always makes a nice refreshing end to any dinner party and the flowers make it really pretty

A dish of snow. Making this is a bit messy, but children would love to help to make an interesting table setting for Christmas dinner

Georgian beetroot pancakes. Do not be put off by the colour of these pancakes. The brandy really works well with the beetroot

A fancy dish of herrings. It is a bit fiddly to get their tails to stick up, but this dish looks very impressive when brought to the table

Pistachio cream. This is delicious but very rich, so only serve a small portion

Chantilly basket. As soon as I found this recipe I could not wait to make it. It is a real talking point around the dinner table

Oranges filled with jelly. How is it the simplest things are always the best? It is so easy to make these jelly segments, but they look really impressive and are great for a children's party

Mrs Beeton's Christmas cake with frosted holly leaves. This cake keeps very well and is more of a ginger cake containing fruit than a Christmas cake. Very good spread with butter for tea in the new year though!

Baked fruit pudding. This recipe is really as good as it looks and fat free too.

Post-war prawn cocktail. It may be a bit old fashioned, but this dish takes a lot of beating as a starter to any dinner party

Cocktail party nibbles. If you get all the ingredients together these take no time at to assemble and are seriously impressive when served with drinks at a party

Method

1. Put the biscuits in a glass bowl and pour the sherry over them. Leave it to soak in.

2. Spread the cold custard on top and then put the syllabub on top of that.

3. Decorate with a selection of brightly coloured flowers and crystallized fruits.

Almond Hedgehog

This is good, but rather expensive to make, so halve the quantities if you have only a small party.

1 kg ground almonds

2 tbsp sherry

12 egg yolks

7 egg whites

600 ml cream

50 g sugar

225 g butter melted

150 g flaked almonds

1 packet of green jelly

Method

1. Mix the almonds with the sherry until it becomes a stiff paste. Beat in the egg yolks and whites.

2. Add the cream, sugar and melted butter.

3. Put in a pan and heat on a very gentle heat, stirring all the time until it is thick enough to form the shape of the hedgehog.

4. On a dish, shape the mixture into a hedgehog and stick it full of flaked almonds to resemble prickles.

5. Make the green jelly and, when cool, pour around the hedgehog.

6. When it is set, stick a few tops of rosemary stems into the jelly to make it look like grass.

Apricot Ice Cream

I still think it is amazing that they had ice cream in the Georgian period!

12 ripe, fresh apricots

175 g icing sugar

600 ml cream

A bowl full of ice and salt

A bowl with a lid on it

A jelly mould with lid

Method

1. Scald the apricots with boiling water and peel and chop them very finely.

2. Mix the sugar, cream and apricots together and put in the bowl with the lid on. Place this into a larger bowl filled with crushed ice and a handful of salt (this makes it slushy).

3. Check it every so often and stir well when the cream gets thick around the edges of your bowl.

4. When the cream is completely frozen, take it out of the bowl and press into a wet mould, putting the lid on when this is done.

5. Put the mould in the bowl of ice, covering it completely, and leave for 4 hours.

6. Serve immediately.

GEORGIAN CHRISTMAS

Roast Turkey

7 kg turkey

Greaseproof paper

225 g butter

Method

After stuffing with chestnut stuffing (see below), smear the turkey with butter and pin the greaseproof paper over the breast. Roast for the time stated on the packaging and for the last 30 minutes, remove the paper and let the skin brown.

Chestnut Stuffing

1 can of chestnuts, chopped finely (or you could get fresh chestnuts, boil them until tender and then shell)

125 g bacon

2 tbsp chopped parsley

1 sprig marjoram

1 sprig thyme

¼ tsp mace

½ tsp nutmeg

Salt and pepper

Method

1. Chop the chestnuts and place them into a bowl. Then add the minced bacon and the rest of the ingredients and work well into a paste. Use this to stuff your Christmas turkey.

Bread Sauce

100 g fine white breadcrumbs

Salt and pepper

50 g butter

1 onion chopped finely

300 ml milk

2 tbsp cream

Method

1. Add the milk, butter, onions and breadcrumbs to a pan.

2. Heat gently until the onions are cooked and the butter has melted.

3. Add the cream and the seasoning to taste, and keep hot until served.

Sausage Shapes to go with the Turkey Dinner

The vegetables to go with this dish seemed, in Hanna Glasse's cookbook, to be anything you wanted, but she did have a recipe for parboiling potatoes, putting them in a pan of hot dripping and shaking the pan until brown. Not much different to what we do today, only we all seem to use tinned goose fat instead of dripping these days.

500 g lean pork

500 g beef suet

1 tsp allspice

1 tsp black pepper

½ tsp nutmeg

1 tsp salt

1 tsp fresh thyme, chopped

1 tsp, fresh marjoram, chopped

2 tsp fresh parsley, chopped

Method

1. Mince the pork in a food processor or a hand mincer if you have one.

2. Add the rest of the ingredients until it is

nicely bound together (it should look like sausage meat).

3. Dust a board with flour and take pieces of the mixture, rolling them into long sausage shapes.

4. Grease an oven tray and arrange the sausages in shapes e.g. O, S, C and X.

5. Bake in a moderate oven for 30 minutes.

6. Arrange the sausage shapes on a platter decorated with fresh parsley and thyme, and serve with the Christmas turkey.

Eighteenth-Century North of England Festive Pie

This is a good recipe for a Boxing Day lunch with some pickle, but you will need a lot of guests to be serving a pie this size!

1 goose

1 partridge

1 pigeon

1 turkey

2 tsp mace

2 tsp black pepper

2 tsp nutmeg

½ tsp ground cloves

1 tsp salt

250 g butter

Hot water pastry (see page 94)

Method

1. See if you can get your butcher to bone all the birds for you.

2. Dust the smallest bird – the pigeon – in the spices and stuff it into the partridge.

3. Dust the partridge and stuff it into the goose.

4. Do the same with the goose and stuff it into the turkey.

5. Place this huge bird into a pre-shaped hot water crust pastry base, covered on top with slices of butter.

6. Pack around the bird some whole onions, parsnips and large chunks of turnip, also covered with the spice mixture and the butter.

7. Put the lid on top and bake for 4 hours in a moderate oven.

8. Take out of the oven and cut away the pastry

lid. Lift the bird onto a platter and arrange it on top of the vegetables.

9. The pastry should be cut into pieces and put on a side plate to be eaten with the meal.

Duke of Buckingham's Pudding with Sherry Sauce

This is a light steamed pudding that would go very well with a rich Christmas dinner.

450 g suet

125 g big raisins chopped

2 eggs

1 tsp nutmeg

1 tsp ginger

125 g flour

50 g sugar

Sauce

75 g melted butter

3 tbsp sherry

3 tbsp sugar

Method

1. Mix all the pudding ingredients together in a bowl.

2. Dampen a large pudding cloth and flour it well all over.

3. Pour the mixture into the middle of the cloth and tie tightly.

4. Drop into a pan of boiling water and simmer for 3 hours.

5. Combine the sauce ingredients and pour over the pudding in dishes.

Christmas Cake with Icing

Here is very large cake from Hanna Glasse's cookbook:

2 kg flour

3½ kg currants

1½ kg butter

1 kg almonds

1 glass of sherry

24 eggs

1½ kg sugar

1 tbsp mace powder

1 tbsp cinnamon

½ tbsp cloves

1 tbsp nutmeg

½ tsp ginger

300 ml brandy

2 oranges

2 lemons

Method

1. Cream the butter and sugar together. Add the eggs one at a time, with a spoonful of the flour with the spices sifted into it.

2. Add the brandy and mix in the fruit and nuts.

3. Add the rind and juice of the oranges and lemons and mix well (no doubt with a huge spoon!).

4. Put in a large round cake tin and bake for 4 hours.

Icing to Ice a Great Cake

These are Hanna's words, not mine!

24 egg whites

450 g icing sugar

Method

1. The recipe calls for beating the egg whites and sugar for 4 hours – this must be a misprint, surely!

2. Then, with a bunch of feathers, spread the icing over the cake and put it back into a cool oven until the icing has dried. Be careful not to let it go brown.

Mincemeat

It is fascinating to learn that the Georgians made the sweet mincemeat that we know today, only they put it into pies between layers of meat.

1½ kg suet

1 kg raisins

1 kg currants

50 eating apples, peeled, cored and chopped finely

225 g sugar

1 tbsp mace

1 tbsp cloves

1 tbsp nutmeg

300 ml brandy

300 ml sherry

Method

1. Chop everything finely and mix it all together. Store in pots until needed.

Mince Pie

Pastry for a large dish

600 g mincemeat (see above)

300 g minced cold roast beef or tongue (or both mixed together)

2 oranges peeled with a knife and sliced thinly

The juice of 2 oranges

Method

1. Line a pie dish with pastry.

2. Put a thin layer of meat at the base, followed by a layer of orange slices, cut very thinly.

3. Top this with a layer of mincemeat.

4. Repeat the layers, finishing with the juice of the orange. Place the pie crust on top.

5. Bake in a moderate oven for 40 minutes until the pastry is nicely crisp. Eat in slices when cold.

Floating Islands

'A pretty dish for the middle of a table to be surrounded with candles.'

1 litre double cream

150 ml sherry

The peel of 3 lemons

125 g icing sugar

3 French rolls

Various coloured jellies

Jellied sweets

Method

1. Put the lemon peel and sugar into the cream and leave for an hour to infuse. Then strain.

2. Add the sherry and beat it well until you have a thick foam on top.

3. Ladle the foam off and put it to one side.

4. Pour the cream onto a large platter.

5. Slice the rolls very thinly and gently place them on the cream, ensuring they are spread out.

6. Spread some jelly onto the roll slices and top with more slices of roll.

7. Repeat this, finishing with a slice of roll.

8. Beat the foam again to make it thick. Drop spoonfuls of the mixture on top of the floating rolls in the pool of cream.

9. Spread sweetmeats around the rim of the platter and surround it with candles. Use it as a centrepiece for your table.

THE VICTORIANS

In the early part of the nineteenth century, most people in the countryside and small towns of Britain ate the food they produced locally. Not until the railway network was built in the mid-nineteenth century did different delicacies sit on the tables of the masses. Simple things we all take for granted, like fresh milk every morning, was only brought about by the new railway distribution systems. Also thanks to the railway systems could fresh sea fish be taken inland each day, and in 1875 the new Billingsgate fish market was built in London as a distribution centre. It was a very grand building for the time and resembled a French chateau, or one of the famous spa hotels in Scotland. The palatial grandeur of the interior was almost created architecturally to resemble a church, so that homage could be paid to the humble fish.

By the 1860s, new roller mills produced white flour free of wheat germ to make cheap bread for the poorer classes to eat. How ironic that, in wanting to emulate the fine white bread of the gentry, they were in fact doing themselves out of the wholesomeness of the bread that they had always eaten in the past. Tinned foods were also developed as a way of bringing cheap products from the empire into the country, but at first they were only a curiosity among members of the rich households who could pay for them – odd, really, when you consider that they had more than enough fresh meat without needing poor-quality, canned Australian substitutes!

Chocolate was reinvented too, from a luxury drink into the solid bar for the mass market to delight in. It was in Switzerland that the Nestle family developed the first milk chocolate. Strangely enough, the popularity of chocolate was promoted by the Quakers, who wanted to give the poor a cheap, alternative drink to alcohol. The Fry family of York and the Cadbury family of Bourneville combined, doing God's work while making a nice profit for themselves at the same time. But to be fair, they did improve the lives of those that worked in their factories immensely, providing them with good housing, schools and health care. The chocolate bar as we know it today was not on the shelves of the sweet shops until 1847, when Fry's produced one cheap enough for the mass market.

Technological innovations in the average kitchen did not really take off until the 1880s, when gas works were built, not only to light the people's streets and homes, but also to fuel their gas cookers. It was an age of so much change – milled flour, baking powder to make lighter cakes and easily used ovens in most homes – that it truly fired the imaginations of the Victorian cooks.

Penny-in-the-slot gas meters made it possible for even the poorest people to use these facilities too. So suddenly there was a huge market for pans, biscuit cutters, ladles, jelly moulds and pie tins to accommodate this new culinary revolution. Towards the end of the century, these items began to be made out of enamel and aluminium, and by the end of the nineteenth century, the refrigerator could be seen in many middle-class homes. It was no longer just the nobility who could enjoy sorbets and ice creams.

Important though this new kitchen equipment was, nothing changed the British diet so much as the food that poured into every port from the far reaches of the British Empire. The Victorian middle classes virtually had the world on their plates as more and more exotic food combinations became a normal part of their diet. The word 'curry', originally 'Kari', was a Tamil word for spiced food that has now become a part of the British vocabulary. This category of Victorian food is so important that I have given it its own sub chapter. But first of all, I will introduce you to some of their recipes without spices.

Prince of Wales Soup

This soup was apparently invented by a philanthropic friend of Mrs Beeton's editor. It was used to feed the poor in a large village to celebrate the coming of age of the Prince of Wales. When I heard of this account, I thought the soup would be a bit special for such an occasion, but as you can see, it is seriously frugal. I suppose the poor at the time would have been grateful for any hot food, but I think she could have put a bit of meat into it!

12 turnips

2 tbsp sugar

2 tbsp strong veal stock

Salt and pepper to taste

2 quarts beef stock

1 loaf of bread

Method

1. Peel the turnips and chop into small pieces.

2. Put them in the stock and simmer gently until tender.

3. Add the veal stock and other ingredients.

Victorian Prince of Wales soup. Very frugal, but O.K. if you want to have a Victorian workhouse party!

4. Cut the loaf into slices and then cut each slice into small circles. Gently drop the circles into the tureen and ladle the soup over them. Care has to be taken not to put the soup in too quickly, or the bread circles would crumple and the appearance of the soup would be spoiled.
NB. It seems that this philanthropic woman was more concerned with the dainty look of the soup than the fact that there is very little nutrition in it!

Brillat Savarin's Fondue

I thought this was only really introduced into Britain when people started going on ski holidays in the 1960s, but Mrs Beeton has proved me wrong, offering two recipes for fondue.

8 eggs

120 g Gruyere cheese

80 g butter

Salt and pepper to taste

Bread cubes

1 bottle burgundy

Method

1. Beat the eggs well in a bowl and add the grated cheese and butter cut into small pieces.
2. Stir the mixture together. Then, set the bowl into a pan of water over the heat until the cheese and butter melts. It should be nice and thick.
3. Then add the seasoning to taste and pour into a sliver or metal dish.
4. Serve immediately with bread cubes for dunking and a glass of burgundy wine.

Macaroni Cheese

This is the Victorian version of one of our all-time favourite British comfort foods. It is interesting that they cook the macaroni in milk and water instead of just water, as we do today.

225 g macaroni

100 g butter

175 g of Parmesan or Cheshire cheese

600 ml milk

1 litre water

75 g fine breadcrumbs

Salt and pepper to taste

Method

1. Bring the milk, water and salt to the boil and drop in the macaroni. Boil until tender.
2. Drain the macaroni and put it in a deep dish.
3. Reserve some cheese for the top and add the rest to the macaroni with most of the butter. Stir well and season with pepper.
4. Mix the remaining cheese with the breadcrumbs and sprinkle over the macaroni.
5. Melt the remaining butter and pour it over the breadcrumbs and cheese.
6. Brown the top under a hot grill and serve immediately.

Toasted Cheese Sandwich

Here is another recipe that I would have classed as a twentieth-century invention. The cheese is incredibly thick in Mrs Beeton's recipe, but it makes me want to go and make some right now!

Slices of brown bread and butter

½ inch thick slices of cheese, either Cheddar or Cheshire

Method

1. Make the sandwiches with the thick slices of cheese and put them on an oven tray.
2. Bake in a hot oven for 10 minutes until the bread it toasted.
3. Serve hot on a napkin and eat quickly.

Bubble and Squeak

This is the original bubble and squeak recipe that does not include potatoes. They were added during the Second World War to make the greens go a bit farther. In my childhood, we used to have this (with potatoes) every Monday with the leftover roast meat from Sunday lunch, and I remember liking it better than the roast itself!

A few slices of cold roast beef

50 g butter

1 large onion, sliced

450 g cooked greens, either cabbage or Brussels sprouts

Salt and pepper to taste

Method

1. Fry the slices of meat in the butter, gently taking care not to dry them out.

2. Lay them on a dish and keep hot.

3. Fry the chopped cooked greens with the onions in a pan with the butter until the onion is soft. Season with salt and pepper.

4. Put on top of the meat and serve at once.

Lark Pie

I put this recipe in just as a curiosity. *Please don't kill any larks to try it for yourself!* The Victorians clearly did not have much of a love for bird-song. You could replace the larks with quail or small pigeons if you wanted to try it.

2 slices of beef (rump steak, beaten well until it is thin)

2 slices of bacon (gammon steak, also beaten until thin)

9 larks (pigeon or quail)

75 g flour

250 g breadcrumbs

The peel of 1 lemon

1 tsp chopped parsley

1 egg

Salt and pepper to taste

2 chopped shallots

300 ml stock

Puff pastry

Method

1. Make the stuffing with breadcrumbs, lemon peel, parsley, and the egg.

2. Stuff the birds with it and roll them in flour.

3. In a deep dish, lay the slices of beef and bacon and put the birds on top of them.

4. Sprinkle with salt and pepper, and add more parsley and chopped shallot.

5. Pour the stock over the birds and then put the puff pastry crust on top.

6. Bake in a moderate oven for 1 hour. During that time, take the pie out and shake it a few times to help make the gravy.

7. Serve very hot – and mind the bones!

Oyster Stew

I could not have a collection of Victorian recipes without oyster stew. Oysters were a very cheap food in Victorian times, and were eaten by everyone – perhaps this is why they are so scarce today!

12 plump oysters

150 ml cream

¼ tsp mace

¼ tsp cayenne

Salt

50 g butter

1 tsp flour

A handful of small cubes of fried bread

Method

1. Wash the oysters well and strain the liquor from the shells. Put in a pan with the oysters and heat slowly.

2. When they just begin to simmer, take the oysters out and take off their beards.

3. Add to the pan the cream and spices, and when it boils add the butter mixed with the flour. Stir continuously until it is smooth.

4. Then put in the oysters and keep them on a low heat until they heat through in the hot sauce.

5. Serve at once sprinkled with the fried bread cubes or sippets, as they were called.

Salmon Pudding

450 g salmon, cooked (just poach it in water for 20 minutes)

225 g breadcrumbs

1 tsp anchovy essence

150 ml cream

4 eggs

Salt and cayenne pepper

Method

1. Fork the cooked salmon, making sure there are no bones or skin on it

2. Mix well with the breadcrumbs and add the anchovy essence, cream and cayenne.

3. Beat the eggs and add them to the mixture.

4. Press the mixture into an ovenproof dish that has been well buttered and bake for 1 hour in a

moderate oven.

5. This can be eaten hot or cold with a salad

Boiled Beef and Carrots

Another stereotypical Victorian meal is boiled beef and carrots, and here is Mrs Beeton's version. As usual, her recipe was for a large number of people, so I have scaled it down somewhat.

2 kg joint of beef silverside

2 tbsp salt

Water

1 kg whole carrots

Method

1. Cover the meat in salt and leave in the fridge for at least 2 days. Then wash off the salt.

2. Get a big pan of water boiling and put the beef in it. Then reduce it to a simmer and cook for at least 3 hours, removing the scum as you cook it.

3. During the last 40 minutes, add 1 kg of peeled whole carrots.

4. Take the beef out of the stock – which can be made into pea soup – and slice the ends off the joint as they will be tough and not pleasant to look at.

5. Put the beef on a large platter surrounded by the whole cooked carrots.

Breast of Lamb with Peas

This cut of meat has gone out of favour, but it is really nice in this recipe, if not too fatty.

1 breast of lamb

4 slices of bacon, thick cut

300 ml stock

1 lemon

A bunch each of mint and parsley

450 g green peas

Method

1. Remove the skin from the breast of lamb and put it in a saucepan of boiling water. Simmer for 5 minutes, and then take it out and put it in cold water.

2. Line the bottom of a casserole dish with the

bacon and put the lamb on top.

3. Peel the lemon with a knife and slice it thinly. Lay it over the lamb.

4. Cover with more slices of bacon.

5. Add the stock, onion and roughly chopped herbs and simmer until tender – about 1 hour.

6. Cook the peas, drain, and put them in a large dish. Lay the bacon and lamb on top and then serve.

Beef Stew a la Mode

A very economical recipe.

1½ kg stewing beef

50 g beef dripping

1 large onion, sliced finely

50 g flour (with 1 tsp salt in it)

2 litres boiling water

12 berries of allspice

2 bay leaves

½ tsp whole pepper

Salt to taste

Method

1. Cut the beef into small pieces and roll in the flour.

2. Put the dripping in a pan and fry the onions in it. When brown, take the onions out.

3. Add the beef and brown it all over.

4. Put into a large pan with the onions pour the water over it and add the rest of the ingredients. Cover the pan and simmer gently for 3 hours.

Beef a la Mode

Not quite so economical!

3½ kg beef

575 g lard

2 thick slices of fat bacon

300 ml vinegar

½ tsp back pepper

1 tsp allspice

1 tsp ground cloves

A bunch of fresh savoury, parsley and thyme (mixed)

3 onions

2 large carrots

1 turnip

1 head of celery

900 ml water

150 ml port

Method

1. Fry the sliced onion in the lard until pale brown.

2. Cut up the other vegetables into small pieces.

3. Chop the herbs finely and mix with the spice.

4. Dip the bacon in the vinegar and then rub into it the herb and spice mix.

5. Lay the bacon on the beef, then roll it up and tie it tightly with string. Rub the rest of the herb and spice mix over it.

6. Put the vegetables, vinegar and water into a pan just a little bigger than the beef joint. Then put the beef in and simmer gently for 5 hours.

7. When it is tender, take the beef out and cut off the string, skimming off any fat from the stock. Add the port wine and let it come to the boil. Then pour this with the vegetables over the beef and serve at once with boiled mashed potatoes.

DESSERTS

Bermuda Witches

This recipe has an intriguing name and includes a very exotic ingredient: Guava jelly.

1 Madeira cake or a plain butter cake

150 g Guava jelly

150 g finely grated fresh coconut (or desiccated coconut that has been left in boiling water for 2 hours and drained)

Method

1. Cut the brown edges off the cake and slice it horizontally.

2. Spread one half with the Guava jelly and sprinkle the coconut on top. Then put the other slice on top.

3. Cut into finger-sized pieces and lay in a sloping fashion on a white napkin on a plate. Dust with sugar and garnish with myrtle sprigs or bay leaves between the slices.

Victoria Sandwich

I had to put in Mrs Beeton's Victoria sandwich recipe, even though it is still seen in most cookbooks today. Interestingly, it was originally

Beef a la Mode. Very tasty stew best made in a slow cooker if you have one

Bermuda Witches. These are simple to make, but look really interesting if you serve them with other cakes at tea time. They taste good too

made in a rectangular cake tin and cut into fingers, rather than made in the round sandwich tins that we are used to today.

4 eggs and their weight in caster sugar, butter and flour

2 pinches of salt

450 g jam or marmalade

Method

1. Beat the butter and the sugar together until it becomes pale.

2. Add the eggs one at a time and beat well.

3. Fold in the flour using a metal spoon.

4. Butter a Swiss roll tin and pour the cake mix into it.

5. Bake in a hot oven for 20 minutes until it is firm and golden brown.

6. When cool, cut it into half and spread the jam or marmalade on one half and put the other half on top and dust with icing sugar.

7. Cut into long, finger-shaped pieces and arrange on a glass plate in a crisscross fashion.

Manchester Pudding

This seems to have gone out of fashion now, but I remember it being made throughout my childhood.

75 g breadcrumbs

300 ml milk

1 strip of lemon peel

4 eggs

50 g butter

50 g sugar

Puff pastry

1 jar of jam

1 tbsp brandy

Method

1. Flavour the milk with the lemon peel by infusing it in the cold milk for 30 minutes.

2. Strain and pour it into the breadcrumbs and put it in a pan. Boil for 2–3 minutes.

3. Add the 4 egg yolks, 2 egg whites, butter, sugar and brandy and stir well together.

4. Line a pie dish with puff pastry and cover it with a thick layer of jam.

5. When the other mixture is cold, pour it over the jam and bake in the oven for 1 hour.

6. Serve cold with a little sifted icing sugar on it.

Chantilly Basket

This is a very elaborate dessert, but well worth it to impress your friends if you have the time!

1 mould (could be a bowl or a cone shape dish)

1 packet of small round macaroons

1 packet of barley sugar sweets

300 ml double cream

50 g icing sugar

450 g strawberries or raspberries

Method

1. Crush the barley sugar sweets and very slowly melt them in a pan over a heat.

2. Carefully dip the edges of the macaroons into the melted barley sugar and glue them together inside your mould. This takes some time, as you need to make sure that they have enough of the toffee to glue them well together.

3. Leave it to set for 2 hours and take your macaroon basket out of your mould.

4. Whip the cream with the sugar, then chop half the strawberries/raspberries and mix with the cream.

5. Just before you serve, pile the strawberry cream into your basket and decorate with whole strawberries on the top. Dust with icing sugar and serve, cutting into the basket for each portion.

NB. Be careful you do not touch the melted toffee when you stick the basket together as it will be very hot and will most likely burn you.

Oranges Filled with Jelly

I could not finish the dessert section for the Victorian period without putting in some jelly dishes. This is a delightful dessert, and very effective on the dinner table.

4 very large oranges

Gelatine to make 600 ml of jelly

Red food colouring

Method

1. Cut a small hole in the top of the oranges and carefully scoop out the contents.

2. Make a jelly out of the squeezed juice of the oranges with added sugar and put red food colouring in half of it.

3. Alternately spoon layers of orange jelly and red coloured jelly into the oranges, leaving it to set between layers. If the jellies start to set, warm them in a bowl of hot water again.

4. When they are filled to the top, leave them overnight to set really well.

5. Cut the oranges into quarters, revealing their striped jelly contents and arrange them on a dish with sprigs of myrtle between them.

NB. This is so simple but so very effective and you could even use three colours of jelly if you wanted.

Apples in Red Jelly

This is simple too, and very pretty.

6 apples

12 cloves

100 g sugar

1 lemon

600 ml water

1 tbsp gelatine

Red food colouring (cochineal if you can get it)

Method

1. Peel the apples and core them. Add two cloves to the hole and as much icing sugar as it will hold.

2. Put them in a large pie dish without letting them touch each other and add the rest of the sugar, the juice of the lemon and the water. Bake in an oven until they are cooked, but do not overcooked them or they will lose their shape.

3. Carefully place the apples in a glass dish, again without letting them touch each other.

4. Strain the liquor the apples have been cooked in and add the rind of the lemon and the gelatine (already dissolved in cold water). Put them in a pan with more sugar if desired and more cloves if necessary. Boil until quite clear, and then add a few drops of red colouring and strain.

5. When cooler, pour around the apples in the glass bowl, leaving the tops of the apples exposed. When cold, garnish the tops of the apple cores with brightly coloured lemon marmalade.

Open Jelly with Whipped Cream

To make this you will need a circular mould or cake tin with a hole in the centre. The Victorians had so many different jelly moulds that there must have been a rather nice income for those companies involved in producing them! No doubt the rich would constantly seek out new sizes and shapes for their many dinner parties.

1½ packets of jelly, preferably dark in colour

300 ml cream

1 glass sherry

Sugar to taste

Method

1. Make the jelly and fill your circular mould, previously soaked in cold water for 1 hour.

2. When set, turn the jelly out onto a dish.

3. Whip the cream with a little sugar and the sherry, and pile into the middle of the jelly.

4. Shape the cream to a conical point and dust with icing sugar on the very top so that it looks like a snow-capped mountain.

VICTORIAN CURRIES

Some of the products that many of us use today originally came from the colonies. One example, of which you may not be aware, is Worcestershire sauce. A Lord Sandys, who was an aristocrat from Worcestershire, apparently came across the recipe when he was the governor of Bengal. In 1835 he is said to have asked two chemists – John Lea and William Perrins – to make some for him from the recipe. This they did, making a jar or two extra for themselves at the same time. But on tasting it, they did not like it at all and put it on a shelf in their cellar and forgot about it. Quite some time later, they found the jars and tasted it again, finding that, after they had matured, the ingredients made a delicious sauce. The exact ingredients are to this day a secret of the Lea and Perrins factory.

One of the most common condiments on any café table today is HP sauce, which was invented to accommodate this new taste for spicy food. A man called Frederick Gibson Garton, who was a grocer from Nottingham, invented the recipe, and because it became popular in one of the restaurants of the Houses of Parliament, he gave it the name HP. Unfortunately his enterprise fell on hard times and he had to sell his recipe and the HP brand to a man called Edwin Samson Moore, the founder of the Midlands Vinegar Company (and the forerunner of the HP Foods Corporation).

Tomatoes originally imported into Britain in the Elizabethan period, suddenly became popular as a basic ingredient for the sauces and chutneys used to accompany curries. When we think of the chutney served with our ploughman's lunch at the pub, it seems so very British, and yet it comes directly from the days of the Raj.

One might think that all the curried foods brought to Britain came from the Indian continent alone. But this is not entirely true, as there were other, subtler, secondary influences on the spicy dishes that landed on British tables during the Victorian Period. This came about when the British sent labourers from India to work in their new plantations in other far-flung parts of the world. They went to Kenya, Uganda, South Africa, Ceylon, the West Indies, Fiji and

Australia, to name but a few. Those Indian labourers took their Indian cuisine with them, and adapted it to the local foods where they now lived. Places like South Africa, for instance, had the perfect climate to produce many lucrative crops, including arrowroot, pineapples, bananas, coffee, etc.

Babotie, a curried minced meat dish, was brought to British tables from the Malaysian migrant workers in Cape Town. The spicy scotch bonnet chilli from Trinidad was added to West Indian curries to give them their fire. The Victorians also added completely alien vegetables to the traditional Indian foods, such as tomatoes, corn, potatoes and kidney beans. When we think of authentic curries at a takeaway, most people would assume a dry potato curry was typically Indian, but, of course, this was a Victorian British invention.

It is believed that the first Indian restaurant in Britain was called The Hindustanee Coffee House in London in 1809. Its owner, Dean Mahomed, had been a cook for a British officer in India and had returned to Britain with him when he retired. He knew just how the British liked their curries – a more general version of his country's regional cuisines. These curries were adapted to suit all British palates, from the very spicy to the very mild. Unfortunately, he was a little ahead of his time and his restaurant closed just three years later. It was not until the later Victorian period, with its vast movement of men and women to and from India and the colonies, that the British population really acquired a taste for a good curry. The bland food of Britain seemed tasteless in comparison to the intricately spiced dishes that they had become so used to. On news of returning home, those Brits would have had their cooks devise curry powder combinations and pastes, so that they could replicate the dishes they knew and loved. Of course, when Queen Victoria herself had Indian cooks in the palace to cook authentic

dishes at palace functions, it then became a must have ingredient for all those who aspired to be associated with the nobility.

Korma – one of our favourite curries – originated in the Islamic courts of the moguls in the eleventh century. In India, Pakistan and Bangladesh, the word 'korma' means a rich banquet dish, and as turmeric is never used in a korma, it keeps its pale, thick, creamy, rich look. The Malaysian kormas are slightly different to the Indian ones, as they have coconut milk in them. This is the korma I like, with its thick coconut sauce and slight sweetness. Korma was the curry of choice for those in Britain that liked the taste of spice, but not the heat of it. In contrast to the korma was of course the madras curry, or the vindaloo that had its origins in Portuguese-occupied Goa. It was generally made of pork and the name comes from the Portuguese words for wine ('vinho') and 'alhos' (garlic). It was probably a simple stew originally, but has now acquired its world famous reputation for being one of the hottest curries you can eat. It is still almost a rite of passage for young men on their first group trips to curry houses in Britain!

One of the most popular Anglo-Indian tastes was the dish of curried eggs. The British were traditionally used to having eggs for breakfast, but while in the tropics they also enjoyed eating curries for breakfast, and so it seems that they combined the two, and curried eggs were born. So popular was this dish, that it was very often eaten for lunch as well as breakfast.

Mrs Beeton's Curry Powder
This curry powder does not have the cumin or turmeric that we usually associate with curry powders such as that in Mr Arnott's recipe, but it is still well worth trying.
125 g coriander seeds
125 g turmeric
50 g cinnamon
2 tsp cayenne

25 g mustard seed

25 g ground ginger

1 tbsp allspice

50 g fenugreek seed

Method

1. Grind all the above in a mortar and store in an airtight tin. Mrs Beeton said that it was just as good to buy curry powder, and was usually cheaper than making it.

Mr Arnott's Currie Powder

Eliza Acton's book included this recipe.

225 g turmeric

125 g coriander seed

125 g cumin seed

125 g fenugreek seed

1 tbsp cayenne pepper

Method

1. Grind all the ingredients in a mortar, as with the recipe above, and store in an airtight container.

Mr Arnott's Currie

What amazed me about this recipe is the selection of meats you can use, from chicken to lobster, and of, course, it was suggested that you could also use the remains of yesterday's calf's head roast!

1 cabbage heart (take all the green leaves off a cabbage until you just have the pale ones)

2 eating apples

The juice of 1 lemon

½ tsp pepper

1 tbsp curry powder (as above)

6 onions

A whole head of garlic

50 g butter

2 tbsp flour

600 ml beef gravy or rich stock made with stock cubes

Cayenne pepper to taste

450 g cooked chicken or mutton or rabbit or lobster or the remains of yesterday's calf's head roast

Method

1. Chop the cabbage heart finely and slice the peeled, cored apples thinly.

2. In a bowl, mix together the cabbage, apples, lemon juice, pepper and curry powder.

3. Fry the sliced onions in the butter until brown, and then add the minced garlic. Add the flour and cook for 1 minute.

3. Add the stock and the rest of the ingredients and bring to the boil, simmering for 30 minutes.

4. Add the meat of your choice and heat through, adding more cayenne if it is not hot enough.

5. Serve with plain boiled rice.

Curried Beef

This useful recipe from Mrs Beeton can be used with left over roast meat.

225 g lean cold roast beef, cut into cubes

75 g butter

2 onions

300 ml of beer

1 dessertspoonful of curry powder

Method

1. Fry the onion in the butter until light brown, and then add the rest of the ingredients. Simmer for 10 minutes.

2. It should be a thick curry, but if it is too dry, add a little more beer or water.

3. Serve in the middle of a bed of boiled rice.

Curried Eggs

8 hard-boiled eggs

1 large onion

1 tbsp flour

1 tbsp curry powder

300 ml chicken stock

The juice of 1 lemon

1 eating apple, peeled, cored and grated

3 tbsp chutney

50 g butter

Method

1. Fry the onion until golden brown in the butter.

2. Add the curry powder and cook for 1 minute.

3. Add the flour and cook for another minute.

4. Pour in the stock and bring to the boil, stirring all the time to thicken.

5. Add the whole peeled eggs, grated apple and chutney.

6. Simmer for 30 minutes for the curry sauce to impregnate the whites of the eggs.

7. Serve with plain boiled rice.

Mutton Curry

From London's Oriental Club in the 1860s.

75 g butter

2 large onions

2 tbsp curry powder

1 tbsp curry paste

1 kg mutton

1 tsp salt

Method

1. Cook the onions in the butter until lightly browned.

2. Add the curry powder and paste to the pan and cook for 1 minute, stirring all the time.

3. Add the cubed mutton and cook until the meat is brown.

4. Pour in 500 ml water or enough to cover it well and add the salt.

5. Bring the water to the boil and, if you have one, put it in a slow cooker for 5 hours. Alternatively, place in a sealed pot on a low oven shelf for 3 hours.

Kedgeree

This dish originally came from Bombay, and was called 'Khichri', consisting of rice, lentils, hard-boiled eggs and scattered with raisins; the fish was served separately. It was adapted into many variations of the recipe below, and was brought back from India to become a favourite breakfast dish during the Victorian period.

150 g smoked haddock

225 g cooked rice

25 g butter

1 tsp mustard

2 hard-boiled eggs

Curried eggs. I loved this recipe it is like a mild curry and I have made it many times since

Kedgeree. This used to be a breakfast dish but make a great dish I think at a dinner party as it is so easy to make and looks good too

1 tbsp parsley, chopped
1 tsp salt
¼ tsp cayenne pepper
1 onion
Method
1. Chop the onion finely and fry until golden in the butter.
2. Mix in the pre-cooked and pre-boned flaked fish, rice, salt and cayenne pepper.
3. Chop the boiled eggs roughly and mix in with the parsley. Serve at once.
NB. A large dish of kedgeree would be kept warm with a candle under it on the sideboard of the average Victorian family, along with bacon, eggs and devilled kidneys.

Curried Cod

This is a lovely, creamy curry. Miss out the cayenne and it is a perfect dish for those who prefer their curry a little milder.
450 g cod fillet (cooked, flaked and de-boned)
75 g butter

1 onion, sliced
300 ml chicken stock
1 tbsp flour
1 tbsp curry powder
150 ml cream
1 tsp salt
¼ tsp cayenne
Method
1. Fry the onions in the butter until brown and add the flaked fish.
2. Add the flour and curry powder and cook for 1 minute. Then gradually stir in the stock.
3. Simmer for 10 minutes and then stir in the cream, seasoning and cayenne.
4. Heat through and serve at once.

Curried Chicken

This is a recipe for chicken curry made with the leftovers of a roast chicken dinner.
225 g cooked chicken (or more if you have it)
2 large onions
1 apple

50 g butter

1 tbsp curry powder

1 tsp flour

300 ml left over chicken gravy

1 tbsp lemon juice

Method

1. Slice the onions and peel, core and slice the apple. Fry in butter until tender.

2. Add the cooked chicken.

3. Add the flour and curry powder and cook for a further 3 minutes.

4. Gradually add the gravy and bring it to the boil.

5. Add the lemon juice and serve in a ring of cooked rice.

NB. Garlic can be added with the onions if desired.

Mulligatawny Soup

This soup or stew can be traced to the beginnings of the East India Company in Madras. It was so widespread in popularity that Mrs Beeton had her own special recipe for it. I think it was the combination of having a soup – the traditional British starter – but with the addition of spices. Atkinson, a captain in the Engineers in 1854, wrote a poem about his trip to India in which he mentioned the soup:

First a sun, fierce and glaring, that scorches and bakes,
Palankeens, perspiration and worry,
Mosquitoes, thugs, cocoa-nuts, Brahmins, and snakes,
With elephants, tigers and Curry.

Then jungles, fakers, dancing girls, prickly heat,
Shawls, idols, durbars, brandy-pawny,
Rupees, clever jugglers, dust storms, slipper'd feet,
Rainy season and mulligatawny.

With Rajahs … But stop, I must desist,

And let each one enjoy his opinions,
Whilst I who in what style Anglo-Indians exist,
In her Majesty's Eastern dominions.

It paints a very vivid picture of the India he knew. A Palankeen was a closed litter carried by four servants, and Brandy-pawny is brandy and water. One thing it does show, though, was how much a part of their Indian life mulligatawny was! The name of this famous soup derives from the Tamil words 'Molegoo' (pepper) and 'tunes' (water), meaning 'pepper water'. It was originally a vegetarian soup, but the British added meat and other ingredients to it to make a whole host of variations in India, Ceylon, and, of course, Britain. It is truly delicious, though. The coconut makes it thick and it is more like a stew than a soup.

1 litre of chicken stock

250 g cooked chicken breast, finely chopped

200 g coconut cream

1 tsp cumin

1 tsp coriander

1 tsp chilli powder

1 small tin tomato puree

2 onions chopped

2 tablespoons chutney

3 cardamom pods

Salt and pepper

2 tbsp butter

Sprig of fresh coriander

Method

1. Fry the onion in the butter until soft.

2. Add the spices to the onions and cook for 5 minutes.

3. Add the other ingredients and bring to the boil.

4. Simmer for 30 minutes and serve sprinkled with chopped coriander leaves.

Mulligatawny soup. I was really surprised at what this original recipe tasted like – a thick Chicken Korma soup. Just my sort of thing as I don't like my curries too hot

Coconut Soup

Here is another exotically inspired Victorian soup from Mrs Beeton.

100 g grated coconut

150 g rice flour

½ tsp mace

1 tsp salt

150 ml cream

2 quarts chicken stock

Cayenne to taste

Method

1. Grate the fresh coconut.

2. Add the coconut to the stock, mace and salt and simmer for 1 hour.

3. Strain and thicken with the rice flour and add the cream and cayenne to taste.

Tomato Sauce (*for keeping*)

To accompany the new fashion for curries, all kinds of catsups, sauces and chutneys were developed. The tomato that was introduced into Britain during Elizabethan times only really became popular during this period as a central ingredient in these essential curry accompaniments.

1 quart tomato pulp (this could be the pulp you buy in cartons or tins)

600 ml vinegar

1 tsp cayenne pepper

50 g shallots

6 cloves garlic

Salt to taste

Method

1. If using fresh tomatoes, bake them in a slow oven until tender and rub through a sieve or liquidize into a pulp.

2. Add the pulp to a large pan with the other ingredients and boil until the garlic and shallots are soft.

3. Take the garlic and shallots out and put them

through a sieve. Then put them back into the pan with the other ingredients. This sauce is ready to use in one week and will keep for 2–3 years.

NB. For a richer sauce, add 600 ml soy sauce and 600 ml of anchovy sauce to every 6 quarts and cook for another 20 minutes.

Mushroom Ketchup

1 kg mushrooms
375 g salt
For each litre of mushroom liquid add:
25 g pepper
1 tbsp allspice
1 tbsp ginger
2 blades of mace
Method
1. Put the mushrooms into a large jar and cover with salt and mix. Put a piece of greaseproof paper over the top and leave them overnight.
2. Strain and boil the liquid for 15 minutes.
3. For every quart of liquid, add the spices and boil for a further 15 minutes. Bottle and use to flavour sauce and curries.

Bengal Mango Chutney

This interesting recipe contains no mangoes, despite its name. Mrs Beeton also says that it was given to an English lady by a native who had lived in India for most of her adult life. Since her return to England, she had become quite celebrated amongst her friends for this excellent Eastern relish. If you look at the ingredients, you will see it was incredibly hot too!

700 g moist brown sugar
350 g salt
100 g garlic
100 g onions
350 g fresh ginger (this is what it says in her book!)
100 g dried chillies
100 g mustard seeds
350 g raisins

2 quarts vinegar
30 large, unripe, sour apples
Method
1. Slowly dissolve the sugar into syrup with a few tablespoons of water.
2. In a mortar, pound the garlic, onions and ginger.
3. The mustard seed must be washed in cold vinegar and dried in the sun (why this has to be done, I can't imagine).
4. Peel the apples and core them, then slice and boil them in 1½ litres of the vinegar until soft. Let this go cold before doing anything else.
5. Put everything else into a large pan with the rest of the vinegar and mix very well.
6. Bottle in the usual way.

NB. Mrs Beeton says: 'This chutney is very superior to any which can be bought and one trial will prove it to be delicious'.

Indian Pickle

This is better known today as piccalilli. This is a very large batch, so scale it down unless you are planning to give it to friends.

4 quarts vinegar
6 cloves of garlic
12 shallots
2 sticks of sliced horseradish (or 2 tbsp horse-radish sauce will do)
100 g bruised ginger
50 g black pepper whole
25 g pepper capsicum
25 g allspice
12 whole cloves
1 tsp cayenne pepper
50 g mustard seed
100 g English mustard (not powdered)
25 g turmeric
1 cabbage (white)
1 cauliflower
A bunch of radishes
250 g French beans
250 g cucumbers or gherkins fresh
250 g small pickling onions

100 g nasturtium seed pods (if you can't get these, large capers will do)

250 g green peppers

Method

1. Cut the cabbage into slices and the cauliflower into branches, and put in a large bowl. Sprinkle with salt and leave for two days.

2. Dry them and put them into a very large jar, with garlic, shallots, horseradish, ginger, pepper, allspice and cloves.

3. Boil enough vinegar to cover them and leave for two days.

4. Then add to the jar the rest of the vegetables to be pickled, making sure they are always covered with vinegar. Leave for two days.

5. Take out the vegetables and pack them into jars without the vinegar.

6. Put the vinegar in a pan and bring it to the boil. Add the cayenne, mustard seed, turmeric and mustard (all of which must have been mixed with a little cold vinegar first).

7. When the vinegar is boiling hot, pour it over the pickles in the jars.

NB. This pickle will keep for years and was a real favourite with cold meat, but has gone out of fashion these days.

INDIAN DESSERTS

Here are some pudding recipes from Mrs Beeton with Indian names. The ingredients are far from Indian, so perhaps they were favourite British recipes enjoyed by those living far away from home.

Delhi Pudding

4 large apples

A little grated nutmeg

1 tsp minced lemon zest

2 tabs sugar

150 g currants

350 g suet crust pastry (half suet to flour with a pinch of salt)

Method

1. Peel, core and slice the apples and put them in a saucepan with the nutmeg, sugar and lemon peel.

2. Cook until soft and then leave to go cold.

3. Roll the suet crust pastry into a large rectangle.

4. Spread the apple mix over it and sprinkle with currants.

5. Roll it up and seal the edges with water.

6. Flour a large, damp pudding cloth with a generous amount of flour and put the pudding onto it. Tie it well.

7. Boil in a large pan for 2 hours and eat at once with custard.

Indian Fritters

3 tbsp flour

4 egg yolks

2 egg whites

Lard for frying

Jam for serving

Method

1. Put the flour into a bowl and add enough boiling water to make a stiff paste.

2. Leave it to cool and then break into it the egg yolks and the egg whites. Beat until smooth.

3. Have a pan of boiling lard or butter ready and drop spoonfuls of the batter into it. Cook until light brown. They should rise when they are cooked, like balls.

4. Serve immediately with a spoonful of jam on each fritter.

Indian Trifle

This seems a little fiddly, but is a very pretty dish on the table.

1 quart milk

The rind of a large lemon

Sugar to taste

5 heaped tbsp rice flour

25 g flaked almonds

300 ml ready-made custard

Method

1. Simmer the milk and lemon rind together

for 5 minutes and stir in the rice flour (previously moistened with milk and enough sugar to sweeten it).

2. Boil and then simmer for 5 minutes, stirring all the time.

3. Take it away from the heat and cool. Then pour onto a broad, shallow glass dish.

4. Let it go completely cold and then cut star shapes carefully out of the rice pudding, filling in the holes with cold custard.

5. Decorate the custard with flaked almonds stuck in upright.

6. Decorate the rice with coloured pieces of jelly or preserved fruits.

Pineapple Fritters

Mrs Beeton says that this is a very elegant dish, and would have been cheap to make because of all the pineapples arriving on ships from the West Indies.

1 small pineapple
1 small wineglass of brandy or liqueur
50 g icing sugar
300 ml batter (made with 300 ml milk, 1 egg and 100 g flour)

Method

1. Pare the pineapples and core and slice thinly.

2. Soak these in the liqueur or brandy and sugar for 4 hours.

3. Make the batter and dip the slices into it. Fry them in boiling lard for 5 minutes until they are brown on both sides.

4. Place onto a white doyley and sift icing sugar over the top. Serve immediately.

VICTORIAN CHRISTMAS

Roast Goose

5 kg goose
Stuffing
3 onions
4 large cooking apples
2 tbsp sage leaves

½ tsp pepper
½ tsp salt
2 tbsp melted butter
Gravy
500 ml stock (giblets and wing tips of goose boiled in water for 1 hour to make stock)
1 onion
2 carrots
2 tbsp goose fat
1 bay leaf
3 sprigs parsley
1 sprig thyme
1 sprig marjoram
Salt and pepper to taste

Method

1. Rub the outside of the goose and inside the cavity with salt.

2. Chop the onion and fry with the butter, salt, pepper and sage until transparent.

3. When cooked, chop the apple and add this to the mixture. Then stuff the bird with it.

4. Put the bird on a wire rack in a roasting tin and bake in a hot oven for 20 minutes. Then reduce the heat and cook for 20 minutes per 500 g. Half way though the cooking time, turn the goose over and drain the fat from beneath the rack.

5. While the goose is roasting, make the gravy by adding some goose fat to a pan along with the onion and carrots.

6. Cook until browned, and then add the stock and seasoning. Simmer for 1 hour.

Roast Turkey and Sausage Meat Stuffing

The Victorians really invented the roast turkey Christmas dinner we eat today, including the stuffing, bread sauce, sausages, thick gravy and all the usual vegetables.

7 kg turkey
Flour for dusting
225 g melted butter
Greaseproof paper
Salt

Stuffing

175 g lean pork

175 g fat pork

50 g breadcrumbs

1 tbsp chopped sage

½ tsp mace, powdered

1 tsp salt

¼ tsp pepper

1 egg

Method

1. Make the stuffing by chopping the pork meats finely and mix well with the other ingredients. Stuff the bird with the stuffing and spread the breast with butter.

2. Roast the turkey for the time stated on the packaging, but instead of covering it in foil, cover it in buttered greaseproof paper and baste with the juices every half an hour.

3. For the last 15 minutes, take off the paper and dust with seasoned flour and ladle over the melted butter. This will crisp up the skin nicely.

4. Serve with bread sauce, sausages and all the trimmings.

Brawn

I am repeating the brawn recipe from the Elizabethan period here, as it was just as popular with the Victorian country folk for Christmas as it was during Elizabeth's reign.

1 pig's head, cut into halves

300 g salt

8 onions

2 tbsp dried sage

1 tbsp peppercorns

½ tsp pepper ground

Method

1. Rub the salt all over the halved pig's head and put in a pan. Leave for 2–3 days.

2 Take the brains out and poach them in water for about 30 minutes (these would disintegrate if cooked for longer).

3. Wash all the pieces well with cold water and put in a large pan, just covering them with water. Add the peppercorns and simmer for 2–3 hours until the meat is coming off the bones.

3. Lift the pieces onto a tray and leave the liquor to cool.

4. Take all the meat off the bones and mince it with a fork. Add the sage, chopped onion and pepper and salt to taste (some liked to keep the eyes and brains whole as a centrepiece, but that is up to you. If you don't want to do this, just mince the eyes along with the meat and the poached brain).

5. Remove the fat from the surface of the liquor and strain the liquor through a thick cloth.

6. Return 4 litres of this liquor to the cleaned pan and add the meat, onion and sage.

7. Simmer for 15 minutes, stirring frequently.

8. Have ready about a dozen pie dishes and basins and pour the mixture into them, leaving it to go cold.

9. When it is turned out, it is covered by a lovely glossy jelly and tastes delicious with applesauce and bread.

Mrs Beeton's Unrivalled Christmas Pudding

This is enough to make at least four big puddings, so you can either divide the quantities or make the entire batch and give them as Christmas presents.

675 g muscatel raisins

675 g currants

450 g sultanas

1 kg soft brown sugar

1 kg breadcrumbs

16 eggs

1 kg suet

175 g candied peel

The rind of 2 lemons

25 g nutmeg

25 g cinnamon

25 g ground almonds

150 ml brandy

Method

1. Mix all the dry ingredients together.

2. Beat the eggs together and add the brandy.

3. Mix the remainder of the ingredients with the eggs.

4. If you are going to make a huge pudding for a lot of people, dampen a large pudding cloth and butter and flour it very well. Put the pudding mix onto it and tie it tightly, boiling for 6–8 hours. If you are going to divide it into four, use either four pudding cloths for a traditional round pudding or greased and floured pudding basins. These will still need at least 3 hours' cooking time.

5. Cover with a fresh cloth when cold and store until Christmas Day.

6. Place in a fresh, dampened and floured cloth and boil for another 3 hours for the big pudding, and another hour for the smaller ones.

Plum Pudding Sauce

1 wineglass of brandy
50 g butter
1 glass Madeira
50 g icing sugar to taste
Method

1. Put the sugar and butter along with a little of the brandy into a basin and stand in a warm place until the butter has melted.

2. Add the rest of the ingredients and keep warm until ready to serve over the pudding.

Vegetable Plum Pudding

To show the discrepancy between social classes in Victorian Britain, here is a recipe from Eliza Acton's book for poor people's Christmas pudding. This recipe is said to have been enough to feed 16 people.

450 g boiled and mashed potatoes
225 g boiled and mashed carrots
450 g flour
225 g suet
350 g sugar
450 g currants
450 g raisins
2 tsp nutmeg
2 tsp mixed spice

½ tsp salt
2 eggs
1 glass of either brandy, sherry or stout
Method

1. Mix together the mashed, cooked potatoes and the carrots.

2. Mix in the flour and the rest of the ingredients (if adding brandy or spirits, then add 50 g breadcrumbs to the mix).

3. Flour a dampened pudding cloth well and put the mixture into in the middle. Tie tightly.

4. Put into boiling water and boil for 4 hours. NB. This pudding would probably have been served with a sweet white sauce instead of the usual brandy sauce.

The Victorians seem to have eaten the old mincemeat pies with meat in them alongside the fruit ones we all know and love today. Mrs Beeton has both mincemeat recipes together as festive pies. They must have had some way of telling the difference between the two types, for it would not have been a very pleasant experience to bite into a mince pie thinking it is going to taste sweet, only to find that it has beef in it! I experienced this myself when a Cornish family invited me for Christmas tea. I was given a cold mince pie and asked if I would like clotted cream on it. I said yes, as I love clotted cream on mince pies. But when I bit into it, I discovered that it was made of cold minced beef! There were no spices or fruit or even onions in it, just minced beef in a little pie case and eaten cold with clotted cream! I thought this might have been just the tradition of that particular family, but a few years later I went to another local party and was given the same thing. They are obviously an acquired taste, as I personally don't think that cold beef in pastry with clotted cream is particularly appetising!

Mrs Beeton's Mincemeat (*fruit mincemeat*)

3 large lemons

2 large apples

450 g raisins

450 g currants

450 g suet

1 kg moist brown sugar

75 g sliced citron (whole candied peel)

1 teacup of brandy

2 tbsp orange marmalade

Method

1. Grate the rind of the lemons and squeeze out the juice (boil the remainder of the lemon until it is tender and then chop it very finely and add it to the bowl).

2. Bake the apples after they have been peeled and cored, and then add to the bowl.

3. Add the rest of the ingredients and mix well.

4. Store in jars and it will be ready to use in two weeks.

Mrs Beeton's Christmas Cake

This is a very different cake to the one we know today. The huge amounts of fruit seem to be reserved for the pudding and the mince pies, as this cake is actually a ginger cake with only a little fruit in it. Or perhaps it is a fruity version of our Twelfth Night cake.

1.25 kg flour

250 g melted butter

300 ml cream

300 ml treacle

250 g moist brown sugar

2 eggs

25 g ginger

225 g raisins

1 tsp bicarbonate of soda

1 tbsp vinegar

Method

1. Melt the butter.

2. Put the flour, sugar, ginger and raisins into a bowl.

3. Stir the butter into the dry ingredients with the cream, treacle and whisked eggs and beat the mixture well.

4. Dissolve the soda in the vinegar and add to the mixture.

5. Put the mix in a buttered mould or tin and bake in a moderate oven for 2 hours or until firm to the touch.

Frosted Holly Leaves

This is a lovely way to decorate a festive table.

Sprigs of holly

Melted butter

Icing sugar and caster sugar mixed

Method

1. Pick the holly leaves from their stalks and dry them near the fire (not too near, or they will shrivel).

2. Dip the leaves in the butter and sprinkle over the mixed sugars.

3. Put them near the heat again to dry, then decorate the table with them or use pins to stick them into the base of a candle. Sit the candle on a large plate, also decorated with the leaves.

NB. Do not let the candle burn low enough to touch the leaves or they will catch fire.

Hot Christmas Punch

300 ml rum

300 ml brandy

125 g sugar

1 large lemon

½ tsp nutmeg

600 ml boiling water

Method

1. Rub the sugar over the lemon peel until it has taken all the zest into the sugar.

2. Add the lemon juice mix to the brandy, rum and nutmeg.

3. Add the boiling water and serve.

THE SECOND WORLD WAR

Wartime shortages led to the creation of the Ministry of Food, the Dig for Victory campaign and powdered eggs. Marguerite Patten was instructed to invent interesting and tasty recipes for British housewives with very restricted larders. The interesting thing was that, because it was a very restricted diet, some of the poorer people in Britain had never eaten so well! The state took control of their diets, rationing sugar (which was very hard to get) and fat, and forcing people to eat wholegrain bread – for many, this would have been a healthier diet than the one they were used to. To supplement their diets, people dug up their lawns and grew potatoes and cabbages in their flowerbeds, providing their own, very locally sourced vegetables.

Just to highlight the difference between the British and the Americans during the war, I will relate a fascinating story. The American troops stationed in Britain brought with them their favourite chocolate bar – the Hershey bar – as part of their rations. Chocolate bars were so important to the American soldiers that the American government had their food technicians adapt the bar so that it did not melt too easily when the troops went into the tropics during the war. Having government food scientists spend their time developing a chocolate bar that does not melt seems worlds apart from what was happening in Britain, as the Ministry of Food was trying its best to get the nation enthusiastic about dried eggs!

The Ministry of Food, with its seemingly endless leaflets on cooking for the Home Front, was designed to do three important things. Firstly, to keep the morale of the British people high by giving them a challenge in the kitchen, the challenge being to make relatively normal meals while handicapped by rationing. Secondly, it was to make the housewife feel as if she was in some way contributing to the war effort by being inventive in the kitchen. Thirdly, and most importantly, because the government did not know how long or how bad the food shortages were going to become, they needed to ensure that the health of the next generation did not suffer as a consequence. They were only too well aware of the problems that bad diet could have on the development of children from the depression of the 1930s. They knew that children's diets, whilst not exactly fun, should include all their nutritional requirements, and invented such cartoon characters as Potato Pete and Doctor Carrot in order to try and make it fun for the children to eat their vegetables. The character of Popeye had been used in much the same way during the 1930s to make spinach seem attractive to young children. Other posters showed a silhouetted child drinking from a mug and the backbone of the child was a bottle of milk. The caption read 'Milk: the backbone of young Britain'.

So the efforts of the Ministry of Food during the war made the diet of the poorer people of Britain better than it had ever been before. Cheap loaves of unhealthy white bread were replaced by wholemeal bread, sweet, stodgy and fatty puddings were taken out of the diet due to the short supply of sugar and fat. Some evacuee children, sent to the country from the inner cities, drank fresh milk on a regular basis for the first time in their lives.

At the same time, there were posters saying: 'A clear plate means a clear conscience'. This attitude to food continued well after the war and has not helped those of us trying to lose weight! My mother in the 1950s would constantly tell me about the starving children all over the world, and how I had to clean my plate or it would mean I was ungrateful for the food I was given. How in hindsight my eating all my food would really make a difference was ridiculous, but I still feel a sense of guilt if I throw any food away. I have resolved this problem now by keeping three hens that eat all the leftovers, thereby recycling my waste into fresh eggs!

One thing those wartime days could teach the cooks of today is the ingenious use of leftovers. All too often we go to the supermarket and buy all sorts of ingredients for the week's meals – usually for at least seven dinners in my case. In my mother's day, a good Sunday roast would make one or maybe two different leftover meals on Monday and Tuesday, thereby saving a considerable amount of money and resources. You will see that there are a lot of leftover recipes in this section which, in our times of credit crunch, might be useful to revive.

Before I list some of the recipes used in wartime Britain, I would like to list some recipes from my own mother's cookbook during the war. My father was an engineer in Denmark before the war. Just weeks before the war broke out in September 1939, he came home to Britain to marry my mother – his fiancée of seven years. They took their honeymoon in Denmark and my father had just gone back to

work when the war broke out. They did not get out in time and were soon captured by the German soldiers. My mother was taken to an internment camp for British women and children in Jutland and my father, for some unknown reason, was moved around various camps in Europe throughout the war. So after just a few weeks of marriage, they were both separated and were prisoners of war for five years. My mother obviously had access to Red Cross parcels but, looking at the recipes from her own handwritten book named *Cookery Book, Denmark 1942,* she seemed to have had more ingredients to hand that weren't so readily available in Britain at the time.

Even though this chapter is about British wartime food, I think the recipes of a small British group in Jutland, cooking in their prison camp during the war, still fit well into this section. I had been brought up with stories of 'the camp' at Store Grundet, Vejle by my mother. After her death, I had the opportunity to go to an archaeology conference in Denmark in 1995, and so I contacted a local historian and told him about my mother's wartime story. He arranged for me to visit the place where my mother had been a prisoner.

My Mother's Second World War cookbook

Christmas and
New Year Greetings

Store Grundet
Vejle

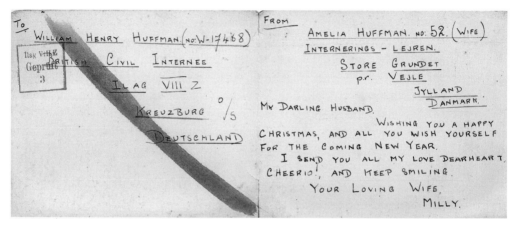

Clockwise, from top left A Christmas card from my mother's camp (a fellow prisoner did the line drawing of the camp)

My Mother with the camp building in the background

The inscription inside the Christmas card from my mother to my father

It has been empty since the war, and was in the process of being renovated. I spent the afternoon matching up photographs of my mother with parts of the buildings and taking pictures of what it is like now. I had always been intrigued by pictures of my mother on a beach at the time and was told by the historian that if it was a nice day, the German soldiers would take the women and children to the beach for the day in a truck. They were just ordinary soldiers, and I remember my mother saying that they were always very considerate and kind to them. What I did not know, and what my mother never told me, was that when

the SS found they were losing the war, they arrived in the village and told the solders to kill all the inmates of the camp. The soldiers refused to do this and fought the SS troopers off until the British troops came in to relieve them. It must have been a very scary time for my mother, which is why she probably never told me about it. It just goes to show that on both sides in the middle of a war, most people do what their conscience tells them is right, no matter what the consequences. The soldiers from my mother's camp had lived with them for five years and were not going to kill them just before they were about to go home.

Curry or Paprika Stew

1 onion
1 tbsp of curry powder or paprika
350 g meat
2 tbsp dripping
1 tbsp corn flour
Salt and pepper
450 g boiled potatoes

Method

1. Fry the onion in the dripping in a stewing pan.
2. Add the meat to the pan with the curry powder or paprika.
3. Mix the corn flour with some water and add to the water in the pan.
4. Cook until the meat is tender.
5. Add the salt and pepper and a little sauce if preferred (she does not state which kind of sauce, but I should image it might have been tomato sauce, as she lists it as an ingredient in another recipe).
6. Serve with boiled potatoes.

Hot Beetroot

450 g beetroot
The juice of 1 lemon
1 tbsp sugar
2 tsp salt

Method

1. Cook the peeled and diced beetroot until tender.
2. Add the lemon juice and sugar and serve hot as a vegetable.

Beef Pinwheels

450 g minced beef
6 tbsp breadcrumbs
400 g mashed potatoes

Beef pinwheels. Be careful when rolling these out or you might loose the peas!

400 g peas

2 tbsp tomato juice (or tomato sauce)

1 egg

1½ tsp salt

¼ tsp pepper

2 tbsp melted butter

Method

1. Mix together the beef, breadcrumbs, tomato juice or sauce, egg, salt and pepper.

2. Roll this out between two sheets of grease-proof paper to 6 in x 12 in, and ½ in thick.

3. Cover half with potatoes and half with peas.

4. Roll up and cut into 1 inch thick slices.

5. Brush with butter and bake for 12 minutes on each side until brown.

Tomato, Cheese and Rice Bake

2 hard-boiled eggs

400 g thinly sliced tomatoes

125 g grated cheddar cheese

300 ml of white sauce (made with milk, corn flour, butter and salt and pepper)

225 g cooked rice

1 tbsp curry powder

Method

1. Grease a dish and place a layer of the sliced tomatoes on the bottom.

2. Cover with sliced hard-boiled eggs.

3. Sprinkle on the curry powder and then half the cheese.

4. Spread over half the white sauce then top with the cooked rice.

5. Top with the rest of the sauce and the cheese.

6. Cover with a piece of greaseproof paper and bake in a moderate oven for 30 minutes.

Bacon and Potatoes

225 g bacon

450 g potatoes

50 g butter

1 tbsp flour

Method

1. Fry the bacon in the butter in a pan for 5 minutes (but don't brown it).

2. Cut the potatoes into very thin slices and cook in the pan, with the lid on, over a low heat until done, stirring every so often. Serve at once.

Brown Stew and Dumplings

225 g stewing beef

3 carrots

3 small onions

2 tomatoes

1 celery heart

1 tsp gravy browning

Salt and pepper

1 tbsp potato flour

For dumplings

125 g flour

1 large potato, grated

1 tsp baking powder

1 tsp salt

Method

1. Chop all the vegetables finely and bring them to the boil, simmering until tender.

2. Thicken with potato flour and put in the gravy browning to improve the colour.

3. Mix the dumpling ingredients together and moisten with water.

4. Make balls the size of golf balls and drop them into the stew.

5. Cook with the lid on for another 30 minutes until they are done.

Lemon Fromage

2 eggs

50 g sugar

The juice of 1 lemon

The peel of half a lemon

2 tsp powdered gelatine

Method

1. Mix the egg yolks and sugar well.

2. Melt the gelatine with a little hot water and mix with the lemon juice and rind.

3. Beat the egg whites until stiff and fold all the ingredients together. Leave to set.

Strawberry Pie

Pastry shell

250 g flour

75 g butter

¼ tsp baking powder

½ tsp salt

3 tbsp water

Filling

1 quart strawberries

300 ml water

3 tbsp corn flour

1 tsp lemon juice

300 ml sugar

300 ml whipped cream

Method

1. Mix the dry ingredients together until they are like fine breadcrumbs and bind with water to make pastry dough.

2. Line a pie dish with it, making a twisted pattern at the edges to keep the shape.

3. Prick with a fork and bake in a hot oven for 10 minutes.

4. Line the cooled pastry shell with the strawberries, reserving 1 cup of berries for the glaze.

5. Simmer the berries for the glaze in the water for 3–4 minutes and mix in the corn flour and sugar.

6. Simmer until clear and thickened, and add the lemon juice. Leave it to cool slightly.

7. Pour over the berries and chill thoroughly.

8. Decorate with a border of the whipped cream.

Swiss Roll

2 eggs

50 g flour

50 g corn flour

125 g sugar

1 tsp baking powder

1 jar of jam

A pinch of salt

Method

1. Mix all the ingredients together (except the jam) and beat well.

2. Bake in a greaseproof paper-lined Swiss roll tin in a hot oven for 10 minutes.

3. Turn out onto a sugared board.

4. Spread with jam and roll up quickly.

5. Trim the ends and sprinkle with more sugar.

MINISTRY OF FOOD RECIPES

Here are some recipes from the Ministry of Food leaflets distributed during the war:

Lamb Chop Hot Pot

This is a very economical meal, and very tasty too.

25 g lard or cooking fat

50 g chopped onions

4 lamb chops

450 g thinly sliced potatoes

225 g sliced carrots

225 g sliced turnip or swede

A pinch of mixed herbs

2 tsp salt

¼ tsp pepper

300 ml water or stock

225 g shredded cabbage

Method

1. Melt the fat and fry the onions and chops on both sides for about 5 minutes.

2. Lift out the chops and put in the mixed vegetables, herbs, salt and pepper and stock or water. Stir.

3. Put the chops back on top.

4. Cover the pan and simmer for 30 minutes.

5. Add the cabbage and cook for a further 10 minutes. Serve immediately.

Meat Curry

This is a very interesting curry and well worth trying. I really like it with the macaroni, as suggested in the recipe.

1 small onion

1 medium-sized eating apple

60 g dripping or lard

450 g beef or lamb

1½ tbsp curry powder

4 tbsp flour

½ tsp dry mustard

350 ml stock or water

1 tsp sugar

1 tbsp chutney

1 tbsp marmalade

1 tsp black treacle

2 tsp salt

Method

1. Chop the onion and apple and fry in the melted dripping.

2. Add the meat cut into 1 inch cubes and fry until browned.

3. Remove the meat from the pan and work in the curry powder, mustard and flour.

4. Cook for 2–3 minutes and add the liquid gradually. Bring to the boil, stirring all the time.

5. Add the sugar, chutney, marmalade, black treacle and salt.

6. Put the meat back in and simmer for 1–1½ hours, or until tender.

7. In place of rice, serve with macaroni, barley or potatoes.

Mince-in-the-hole

125 g minced meat (beef, pork or lamb)

1 leek, finely chopped

2 tsp mixed herbs

1 tsp salt

A pinch of pepper

25 g cooking fat

Batter

125 g flour

1–2 eggs

½ tsp salt

A pinch of pepper

300 ml milk

Method

1. Mix together with your hands the mince, leeks, herbs and seasoning.

2. Form into small balls.

3. Melt the fat in a baking try and add the meatballs. Put in the oven to brown.

4. Make the batter by mixing the flour, eggs, seasoning and milk together.

5. When the meatballs are brown, pour over the batter and return to the oven for 30 minutes until the batter is cooked and brown.

Hamburgers in Brown Sauce

This hamburger recipe is good and spicy, and quite unusual to our modern taste buds, being served in gravy instead of in a roll with lettuce.

Hamburgers

225 g minced beef

125 g stale bread (soaked and squeezed)

A pinch of herbs

2 tsp salt

¼ tsp pepper

¼ tsp English mustard

4 tsp Worcestershire sauce

2 tbsp finely chopped onion

1 egg (optional)

Sauce

50 g dripping

1 small onion, chopped

60 g flour

600 ml stock or water

Gravy browning

½ tsp salt

¼ tsp pepper

1 tsp chutney

1 tsp sugar

2 tbsp diced carrots

2 tbsp diced potato

Method

1. Mix all the hamburger ingredients together and shape into 8 rounds.

2. Fry in a shallow pan until browned, but not cooked through.

3. Remove the hamburgers from the pan.

4. Fry the onion until brown, add the flour and mix well.

5. Add the liquid gradually, stirring all the time until the sauce boils.

Beef and lettuce salad with mustard sauce. The mustard sauce is like homemade salad cream. If you like corned beef you will love it

6. Add the other ingredients and the hamburgers and cover. Simmer for 15–20 minutes.
7. Serve with potatoes.

Corned Beef was one food that everybody was provided with at least once or twice a month. It was very useful and could be made to go a very long way. Here are just a few recipes that use corned beef as a main ingredient, rather than eating it in a sandwich with English mustard as we do today.

Beef and Lettuce Salad and Mustard Sauce

4 tbsp flour
1 tbsp mustard powder
1 tsp salt
½ tsp pepper
300 ml water
1 tbsp finely chopped onion
1 tbsp vinegar
125 g corned beef (a small can is about 200 g, so you can see how little was used)
1 medium lettuce
A few radishes and cooked peas to garnish
Method
1. Mix the flour, mustard, salt and pepper to a smooth cream with a little of the water, and then add the onion.
2. Boil the rest of the water and pour on to the blended mustard powder. Return to the pan and bring it to the boil.
3. Boil gently for 5 minutes, and then beat in the vinegar and allow it to cool.
4. Flake the corned beef and shred the lettuce, and mix these ingredients with the cold sauce.
5. Line a bowl with the outside leaves of the lettuce and pile the filling into the centre.
6. Garnish with slices of radish and cooked peas.

Corned Beef Rissoles

125 g mashed potatoes
125 g corned beef
125 g brown breadcrumbs
1 medium onion, chopped finely
2 tbsp brown sauce (HP sauce)
A pinch of salt and pepper
Method
1. Flake the corned beef and mix with the other ingredients.
2. Form into small burger shapes and put onto a baking tray.
3. Bake in a moderate oven for 15 minutes until brown, and then serve hot with cooked greens. NB. These rissoles make a good cold lunch snack the next day too.

Corned Beef Hash

200 g corned beef (1 small tin)
400 g mashed potatoes
1 onion
30 g margarine
Salt and pepper
Milk to mix
Method
1. Fry the onion, finely chopped, in a little of the margarine.
2. In a bowl, break up the corned beef with a fork and mix well with the mashed potato. Add salt and pepper to taste.
3. When the onions are lightly browned, add the rest of the margarine and the potato mix and fry, stirring all the time.
4. You will need a heavy saucepan and a wooden spatula. As it starts to brown on the bottom of the pan, stir into the mixture and keep doing this until there is an even mix of browned potato through the hash.
5. Serve at once with brown sauce.

Ministry of Food Curried Corned Beef Balls

1 small tin corned beef
50 g breadcrumbs
2 tbsp sweet pickle
2 tsp curry powder
1 small leek or onion, chopped
1 tbsp gravy
Method
1. Chop the meat up finely and mix with all the other ingredients.
2. Form into four balls.
3. Roll in brown breadcrumbs and shallow fry in a pan until browned all over.
4. Serve hot with gravy or cold with salad.

Macaroni Cheese

Here is an all-time favourite comfort food. This particular recipe is also from the Ministry of Food.

125 g macaroni
3 tbsp flour
300 ml milk
150 ml macaroni water
½ tsp English mustard (not powder)
¼ tsp pepper
125 g grated cheddar cheese (mature is best)
Method
1. Cook the macaroni in boiling salted water until tender for about 20–30 minutes.
2. Drain well. Retain 150 ml of the water and keep the macaroni hot.
3. Blend the flour with a little of the cold milk
4. Boil the rest of the milk and macaroni water, and then pour onto the blended flour.
5. Return the mixture to the pan, stirring all the time, and boil gently for 5 minutes.
6. Add the seasoning and two thirds of the cheese and the cooked macaroni.
7. Mix well and put into a greased pie dish. Sprinkle on the remaining cheese.
8. Brown under the grill and serve at once.

Creamed Sardine Pie

3 tbsp flour
300 ml milk
1 tsp salt
A pinch of pepper

A pinch of nutmeg

1 tsp vinegar

1 can sardines in oil

150 g short crust pastry

Method

1. Blend the flour with the milk and bring to the boil, stirring all the time. Simmer for 5 minutes.

2. Add the seasoning, nutmeg and vinegar.

3. Mix in the mashed sardines with the oil.

4. Line a 6 in flan ring with pastry and add the mixture. Cover with the remaining pastry.

5. Brush the top with milk and bake in a hot oven for 30 minutes.

6. Serve hot or cold with a green salad.

Fish Cakes

225 g cooked fish (any kind)

225 g mashed potato

1 onion

1 tbsp chopped parsley

A few drops of vinegar

1 egg (fresh or dried and reconstituted)

Breadcrumbs

Method

1. Flake the fish finely and check there are no bones.

2. Mix all the ingredients together, apart from the egg and breadcrumbs.

3. Form into fish cakes and dip in beaten egg and breadcrumbs.

4. Shallow fry the fish cakes on both sides until brown. These can be eaten hot or cold with salad or cold in a sandwich for lunch.

Fish Curry

1 small onion

1 small carrot

25 g lard

1 tbsp curry powder

3 tbsp flour

600 ml water or stock

1 tbsp vinegar

1 tbsp chutney

2 tbsp sultanas

1–2 tsp salt

350 g cooked fish

Method

1. Fry the onion and carrot in the fat until tender.

2. Add the curry powder and flour and cook for 1 minute.

3. Add the stock or water and bring to the boil, stirring all the time.

4. Boil gently for 10 minutes, and then add the vinegar, chutney, sultanas, salt and fish.

5. Heat through thoroughly for 5 minutes and serve with mashed potatoes.

Fish Pasties

225 g cooked fish (flaked)

225 g mixed cooked vegetables

1 tbsp vinegar

2 tbsp chopped parsley

150 ml white sauce

¼ tsp pepper

150 g short crust pastry

Method

1. Mix together the fish, vegetables, vinegar, parsley, sauce and seasoning.

2. Roll out the pastry thinly into rounds about 6 inches in diameter.

3. Place a portion of the mixture on one half and dampen the edges.

4. Fold the pastry over and crimp the edges to seal the pasties.

5. Bake in a moderate oven for 30 minutes.

NB. These are very good hot or cold for lunch with a salad the next day.

Pilchard Pie

350 g tin of pilchards in tomato sauce

2 tbsp chopped parsley

2 tbsp chopped onion

50 g mashed potatoes

1 tsp salt

¼ tsp pepper

150 g short crust pastry

Method

1. Mash the pilchards well and mix with the rest of the ingredients.

2. Line a pie dish with the pastry and put in the filling.

3. Cover with the rest of the pastry

4. Bake in a hot oven for 30 minutes.

NB. This is very good cold with tomato sauce or chutney.

Potato and Bacon Cakes

450 g potatoes cooked
6 tbsp chopped onion
75 g bacon
2 tsp Marmite or Bovril
1 tsp salt
A pinch of pepper
Milk and breadcrumbs for coating

Method

1. Mash the potatoes while still hot and chop the bacon.

2. Fry the bacon and then the onion until they are both brown.

3. Add to the mashed potato with the extract and seasoning.

4. Mix well and form into 8 cakes.

5. Coat in milk and breadcrumbs and bake in a moderately hot oven until firm for about 15 minutes.

Savoury Potato Biscuits

50 g margarine
75 g plain flour
75 g mashed potatoes
6 tbsp grated cheese
1½ tsp salt
A pinch of pepper

Method

1. Rub the margarine into the flour and add the other ingredients. Work into a stiff dough.

2. Roll out thinly and cut into shapes. Bake in a moderate oven for 15–20 minutes.

NB. This mixture makes 24 biscuits.

Cheese Pudding

2 eggs
300 ml milk
75 g grated cheese
1 teacup full of breadcrumbs
1 tsp mustard
Salt and pepper

Method

1. Beat the eggs.

2. Boil the milk and stir in the breadcrumbs. Then remove from the heat.

3. Add the cheese, salt and pepper, mustard and beaten eggs.

4. Pour into a dish and bake for 30 minutes until set and brown.

Potato Puffs

450 g cooked mashed potatoes
Salt and pepper
A little flour

Filling

150 g sausage meat (or cooked root vegetables with 25 g grated cheese)

Method

1. Mix cold mashed potatoes with seasoning.

2. Add enough flour to bind the potatoes into dough.

3. Roll out the dough and cut into large rounds.

4. Put a little of the filling on one side of the rounds, dampen the edges and fold over.

5. Bake in a hot oven for 30 minutes.

Dresden Patties

I do not know the connection between Dresden and this recipe. It was devised, however, at a time when fried bread was a normal part of the British diet. Worth trying if you are partial to fried bread!

25 g dripping
50 g flour
150 ml stock or vegetable water
225 g cooked meat, chopped finely (or half meat and half cooked vegetables)
1 tsp salt

Potato puffs. This is real comfort food

Dresden patties. Interesting and very tasty, but the fried bread is a bit rich for our modern tastes

½ tsp pepper

1 tsp Worcestershire sauce

4 rounds of bread cut 2½ cm thick

Chopped parsley

Method

1. Heat the dripping and add the flour. Cook until slightly browned.

2. Gradually stir in the liquid and bring to the boil. Cook for 5 minutes.

3. Add the meat or meat and vegetables.

4. Cut a round into each slice of bread, and cut a smaller round in the middle of each.

5. Fry the rounds and inner circles in hot fat until golden brown.

6. Lay the large rounds in a dish and fill each with the meat and sauce

7. Put the small circle of fried bread on top of the sauce to form a lid, and serve with chopped parsley.

Woolton Pie

This recipe was created by the chef of the Savoy Hotel and named after Lord Woolton, the Head of the Ministry of Food at the time.

450 g diced potatoes

450 g cauliflower

450 g diced carrots

450 g diced swede

3 spring onions

1 tsp vegetable extract (or Marmite)

1 tbsp oatmeal

A handful of chopped parsley

Wholemeal pastry made with 150 g brown flour, 50 g margarine and ½ tsp salt

Method

1. Cook the vegetables with just enough water to cover, stirring to prevent it sticking to the pan.

2. Spoon into a pie dish and sprinkle with the chopped parsley.

3. Cover with a crust of wholemeal pastry.

4. Bake in a moderate oven until the pastry is cooked and serve hot with gravy.

Sausage and Sultana Casserole

450 g sausages

1 large onion

50 g sultanas

1 cooking apple

A pinch of dried mixed herbs

300 ml stock

Salt

Method

1. Fry the sausages and leave on a plate to one side.

2. Fry the onion in the sausage fat.

3. Put the sausages back in the pan and cover with stock.

4. Add the sultanas, herbs and salt. Stir well.

5. Put in a casserole dish and cook in a slow oven for 1 hour.

Vegetable Pie with Cheese and Oatmeal Crust

700 g cooked mixed vegetables

2 tbsp chopped parsley

300 ml stock or water

For the crust

50 g oatmeal

50 g mashed potato

50 g grated cheese

100 g flour

25 g lard or margarine

Salt

Method

1. Place cooked vegetables in a pie dish and sprinkle with the coarsely chopped parsley.

2. Add the stock or water and seasoning.

3. To make the crust, cream the fat and potato together

4. Add to it the cheese, oatmeal, flour and salt and combine it all together.

5. Add a little water if it is too dry – it should be a stiff dough.

6. Roll out the crust to cover the pie dish and put it on top.

7. Bake in a moderate oven for 30 minutes and serve with greens and baked potato.

Vegetable Broth with Sausage Dumplings

125 g self-raising flour (or plain flour and 2 tsp baking powder)

1 tsp salt

25 g suet

1 tbsp chopped parsley

125 g sausage meat

Water to mix for broth

225 g carrots

75 g turnips

75 g onion or leek

125 g chopped outer leaves of a cabbage

225 g potatoes

1 litre stock (chicken if you have it)

Method

1. Chop the onions/leeks, carrots, turnip, cabbage and potatoes into small pieces and put in the boiling stock. Simmer for 30 minutes.

2. Make dumplings by mixing together all the remaining ingredients.

3. Mix with cold water to a stiff consistency and divide into 8 pieces.

4. Roll each piece into balls and dip in flour.

5. After the soup has simmered for 30 minutes, bring it back to the boil and drop in the dumplings.

6. Put the lid on the pan and simmer for 20 minutes until they are cooked.

Baked Fruit Pudding

This is a very hearty and at the same time cheap meal to make – great on a cold winter's day.

600 g stewed fruit of any kind (apple and blackberries are good for this recipe)

125 g stale bread

3 tbsp milk

2 tbsp sugar

Method

1. Put the fruit in an ovenproof dish.

2. Cut the bread neatly into cubes and cover the fruit with it.

3. Sprinkle the bread with the milk and then sprinkle over the sugar.

4. Bake in a hot oven for 20–30 minutes or until the bread crust is golden.

Raspberry Buns

225 g self-raising flour

A pinch of salt

75 g margarine

50 g sugar

1 tsp vanilla essence

150 ml milk (or milk and water)

2 tbsp raspberry jam

Method

1. Rub the margarine into the flour and add the sugar.

2. Mix to a stiff dough with the water and the vanilla essence.

3. Cut the dough into 12 pieces and form into buns. Make a hole in the middle of each.

4. Put a little of the raspberry jam in the holes and pull the dough over it to seal in the jam.

5. Roll lightly in sugar and bake in a hot oven for 10 minutes or until firm to the touch.

NB. Wait until they cool before trying them, as the jam inside will be very hot!

ANZAC Biscuits

ANZAC is an acronym for Australian and New Zealand Army Corps, and was invented in the First World War. These are also known as soldier biscuits. This recipe is from Ministry of Food leaflet 38, and probably intended to show a certain solidarity with the Australian and New Zealand troops in the Second World War.

75 g margarine

75 g sugar

1 tbsp syrup

½ tsp vanilla essence

1 tsp bicarbonate of soda

2 tbsp hot water

75 g flour

225 g rolled oats

Method

1. Cream the margarine and sugar together and add the syrup and vanilla essence.

Raspberry buns. I remember buns like this used to be sold in cake shops and I definitely recall my grandmother making them for tea. I think we should all revive them as they are simple but very, very good

2. Mix the bicarbonate of soda and the water together and add to the margarine and sugar mixture.

3. Add the rest of the ingredients and make a stiff dough.

4. Place a teaspoon at a time of the mixture 2in apart on a baking tray and cook for 20 minutes in a moderate oven.

NB. This recipe makes 36 biscuits.

WARTIME CHRISTMAS

There are lots of references in the wartime literature to mock goose being served at Christmas, but most of the recipes just seem to be layers of onions and potatoes in a dish topped with cheese – not at all goose-like in my opinion! Here is a recipe from the coun-tryside for mock goose, which was a bit more like the real thing.

Mock Goose (Country Style)

1 bullock's heart

2 bay leaves

4 cloves

2 meat stock cubes

4 large onions

1 tbsp corn flour

8 sage leaves

125 g suet or fatty bacon

225 g breadcrumbs

1 egg

Salt and pepper

Dripping

Method

1. Wash the heart and put in a pan with enough water to cover it.

2. Add pepper, salt, bay leaves, cloves and meat cubes.

3. Simmer gently for 4–5 hours until tender.

4. Put to one side until the next day.

5. Take the fat off the stock in the pan and mix together with the egg, chopped onions, chopped sage leaves, suet/bacon and bread-crumbs.

6. Make into forcemeat balls, leaving a little of the mixture to stuff the heart.

7. Put the stuffed heart and the forcemeat balls surrounding it in a baking tin and cover with dripping.

8. Bake in a hot oven for 30 minutes.

9. Strain the stock in which the heart was boiled and use about 600 ml for the gravy.

10. Thicken the stock with corn flour and serve with the heart and baked potatoes.

NB. The leftover heart can be minced the next day and mixed with the gravy to make another dinner. The rest of the stock makes an excellent soup when you add all kinds of vegetables to it.

Savoury Sprouts

225 g sprouts

1½ tbsp flour

150 ml vegetable water and milk mixed

3 tbsp grated cheese

A few drops of lemon essence

½ tsp salt

A pinch of pepper

Method

1. Boil the sprouts in salted water. Keep hot and reserve the liquid.

2. Blend the flour in a little of the liquid and bring the remainder to the boil, stirring all the time. Add the blended flour.

3. Simmer for 5 minutes until thickened and add the cheese, lemon essence and more sea-soning if needed.

4. Add the sprouts and reheat. Serve very hot with the mock goose and baked potatoes.

Ministry of Food Christmas Pudding Recipe (A Good Dark Christmas Pudding)

500 g plain flour

½ level tsp baking powder

½ level tsp nutmeg

¼ tsp salt

½ tsp cinnamon

1 tsp mixed spice

50 g suet or fat

75 g sugar

225–450 g mixed dried fruit

125 g breadcrumbs

25 g marmalade

1 egg

150 ml brandy, rum, ale, stout or milk

Method

1. Sift the flour, baking powder, salt and spices together.

2. Add the sugar, fruit, breadcrumbs and suet.

3. Mix with the marmalade, eggs and liquid and beat thoroughly.

4. Put into a greased basin, cover with greaseproof paper and steam for 4 hours.

5. Remove the paper and cover with a piece of cloth. Store in a cool, dry place.

6. Steam on Christmas Day for 2–3 hours before serving.

Christmas Cake (Without Eggs)

100 g grated carrots

3 tbsp golden syrup

125 g margarine

1 tsp bicarbonate of soda

½ tsp almond essence

½ tsp vanilla essence

160 g mixed dried fruit

300 g flour

1 tsp cinnamon

1 small teacup of black tea, hot

Method

1. Pour the tea over the dried fruit and leave over-night.

2. Cream the golden syrup and margarine together.

3. Beat in the carrots, the bicarbonate of soda, the essences and spices.

4. Mix in the dried fruit (it will have absorbed most of the tea by now) and then stir in the flour.

5. Line a cake tin with greaseproof paper and add the cake mix to it, spreading it out evenly.

6. Pre-heat the oven to hot and then put the cake in. Turn it down to cool and bake for 3 hours or until firm to the touch.

Ministry Mock Icing for Christmas Cake

2 tbsp water

6 tbsp dried milk

4 level dessertspoons of sugar

Colouring and flavouring

Method

1. Heat the sugar and water gently until the sugar has dissolved.

2. Add the dried milk gradually, beating all the time.

3. Add colouring or flavouring (almond essence is nice).

NB. For chocolate icing (for chocolate log) use 5 tbsp dried milk and 1 tbsp cocoa powder instead.

Ministry of Food Mincemeat

225 g mixed dried fruit

125 g apples

125 g sugar

125 g margarine or suet

½ tsp mixed spice

½ tsp cinnamon

1 tsp nutmeg

¼ tsp salt

6 tbsp of brandy, sherry, rum, stout or ale

½ tsp lemon essence

2 tbsp marmalade

A few drops of rum essence (optional)

Method

1. Mince fruit and apples together or chop finely. Add all the other ingredients to the mix.

2. Put into small jars and tie down securely.

Store in cool, dry place.

NB. This will only last 10 days, so only make the amount you will need.

Mock Rum Cream for Mince Pies

2 tbsp custard powder

300 ml milk

25 g margarine

1 tbsp sugar

A few drops of rum essence

Method

1. Blend the custard powder with a little of the cold milk.

2. Warm the rest of the milk in a pan, add the warm milk to the powder paste and return to the pan.

3. Stir over a heat until cooked and thickened.

4. Let it go cold.

5. Cream the margarine and sugar together well. Beat into the cold custard gradually and add the rum essence.

6. Keep in a cool place and serve with hot mince pies.

Christmas Fruit Snow

300 ml water

1 tbsp sugar

1 level tbsp powdered gelatine

150 ml fruit pulp (made from stewed or bottled fruit)

Method

1. Heat the water and sugar together, pour on the gelatine and stir until dissolved.

2. When cool, add the fruit pulp and beat until it is the consistency of whipped cream.

3. Serve in individual glasses or pile into a dish.

Crumb Fudge

At Christmas time, sweets for the children would have been scarce, but this recipe is well worth trying.

2 tbsp golden syrup

50 g margarine

50 g sugar

Crumb fudge. This is surprisingly nice

50 g cocoa
A few drops of vanilla essence
175 g dried breadcrumbs
Method
1. Heat the syrup, margarine, sugar and cocoa gently in a pan until melted.
2. Stir in flavouring and then the breadcrumbs.

3. Mix well and turn into a well greased sandwich tin.
4. Mark into fingers with a knife.
5. Leave for 24 hours, as it improves if kept for a day or two (if it lasts that long, that is!).

THE POST WAR YEARS

When Queen Elizabeth II came to the throne in 1952, Britain was in a sorry financial state. There was still rationing of basics such as sugar, butter, margarine, cheese, cooking fat, bacon, meat and tea which, as you can imagine, was a bit depressing for the homecoming troops who had been relatively well fed on forces' rations. But by 1954, rationing finally ended and, if you had the money, you could buy as much food as you wanted from the shops. Most people, though, due to financial restraints kept to a very similar diet to the one they had had during the war.

In 1955, the first commercial TV station was launched and suddenly all sorts of products were advertised with catchy slogans, such as the Egg Marketing Board's 'Go to work on an Egg'. New sugar-laden breakfast cereals were also promoted with cartoon characters, such as the Snap, Crackle and Pop trio created to advertise Rice Krispies.

Things got back to some sort of normality in the high streets by the late 1950s, and rationing was more or less forgotten. I used to go to the local shops for my mother at that time, and had to tell the man how thickly we wanted our bacon sliced. The butter was cut from a block out of a barrel from Kiel, and cheese was sliced to order with a wire. Everything was wrapped in greaseproof paper or put in a brown paper bag, and apart from tinned food, nothing was pre-packed. On my way home from school, I used to go into the grocer's and ask for a 1d bag of broken biscuits, as all biscuits were sold loose in glass-topped boxes around the shop. During those times, my father had a love of bilberry pie, so when they were in season I would go to the green grocer and ask for 2 lb of the berries, which were put into a brown paper bag. I had to run home quickly then, as the juices would start to seep through the paper and it would soon fall apart! The green grocer's shop was a wonderful, earthy smelling place too. The potatoes were loose and came out of a number of huge hoppers, depending on whether you wanted a floury or waxy variety, and fruits like strawberries and gooseberries were bought with relish when they came into their short seasons. The local shops included a newsagent's, a green grocer's, a baker's, a butcher's, a grocer's, an ironmonger's, a ladies' dress shop and a haberdasher, where you could choose socks and handkerchiefs from wooden drawers.

Then, in 1960, the ladies' dress shop on the corner was sold and in its place there opened a mini-market. This was very exciting for me at the time, as for the first time I was told to take a basket and pick items of food off the shelves for myself. Usually you never touched the food you were going to buy, as the assistants behind the counter would get everything for you. The mini-market was not a big shop, and the aisles between the shelves were quite small, but it was still an amazing novelty to us at the time. The food was all pre-packed and was much cheaper to buy, as it only required one person to take your money, rather than a number of assistants in a variety of small local shops.

The age of convenience had begun, and not long after that, self-service petrol stations began to be built. The number of local grocery stores fell from 150,000 in 1961 to just 60,00 by 1981. It was the beginning of the end for the small local shopkeeper with his personal service and local produce.

The 1960s marked the time of Ideal Home Exhibitions in Britain, where new foods could be sampled and amazing gadgets could be demonstrated. I remember going every year to the Ideal Home Exhibition with my mother and delighting in the endless free samples, from haggis to Mary Baker fudge frosting. Our bags were laden with little goodies to take home, and we spent hours watching demonstrations of new kitchen gadgets. After watching the demonstration, you would wonder how on earth you had ever managed in the kitchen without them. Once home, however, it was never more than a month before they ended up at the back of the cupboard collecting dust. It was a time of plenty, or so it seemed.

TV cooks became popular during those days, as people wanted to be shown how to change their cooking habits. Fanny Craddock was queen during this time, and she always wore evening dresses and frilly aprons on her show. She also ordered her husband Johnny about in her TV kitchen as she prepared just the thing for the formal dinner party. By the end of the decade, new types of TV cooks, like Graham Kerr, also known as 'The Galloping Gourmet', travelled the world showing more exotic foods in a very debonair way. He also used his una-shamed sex appeal to capture large audiences.

People were just starting to take to the air and go to the Costa del Sol in Spain on pack-age holidays, and so to be able to have some Spanish-style dried paella when you got

home was a wonderful thought. There were lots of new instant meals that could provide that exotic flavour simply by pouring boiling water over them. Vesta was the most popular, with TV adverts showing people eating exotic foods from all over the world, before showing you the packet it had come from. Exotic meals like chow mein in a box was one, where you even made your own crispy noodles on top and sprinkled it all with little sachets of soy sauce. The foods were, of course, heavily laced with monosodium glutamate (msg), of which we were unaware at the time. All we knew was that they were incredibly tasty!

In 1961, a new technique for aerating bread to produce the standard sliced loaf was invented. It was called the Chorleywood process, and we were soon on the way to losing our local bakers, many of which were bought up by the huge industrial flour millers, who sold mainly their own large, white, sliced loaves. Companies like Bird's Eye, Ross and Findus started to produce a range of products for the new frozen food industry. Freezer sections of the mini-markets soon became full of fish fingers and frozen peas. No more podding peas from the green grocer's before the Sunday roast for me! We all thought it was wonderful, though. Everything was about labour saving and convenience. In 1974, the Smash adverts on TV for instant dried potato mash showed creatures from Mars laughing at the gardener for digging up his potatoes from the ground, peeling them, boiling them, then mashing with a potato masher. They suggested that anyone who did this was old fashioned and well behind the times.

I can't talk about convenience foods, how-ever, without mentioning the OXO cube, and those cosy family scenes of the 1960s and '70s that portrayed the fun and banter of a typical family dinner. The adverts implied that if you did not sprinkle the magic ingredient – the OXO cube – onto your meal, the food would be tasteless and life in general would be boring.

The first stock cube was actually invented by Baron Leibig, who devised a way to process pulped beef into a cube in 1865, although he was trying to produce a healthy concentrate of meat, and not striving to save the housewife time in the kitchen!

A typical convenience food menu we were taught to serve during domestic science classes at school was as follows: a starter of packet soup, followed by Vesta chow mein and finished with chocolate flavoured Angel Delight and tinned pears. This was, by the way, my school's way of trying to keep up with the times. We were also taught over two years all the basic cooking skills, which I feel would be of great benefit to re-introduce into the curriculum today, as most young people do not even know how to make simple pastry.

The 1960s, though, were all about the modern housewife having more time for leisure activities instead of being 'chained to the kitchen sink', as they used to say. Then the last straw was placed on the camel's back for our homely British food. The Wimpy bar arrived on our high streets, originally an American burger chain named after Popeye's gluttonous friend, Mr. J. Wellington Wimpy, who was always craving a hamburger. His catch phrase was 'I'd gladly pay you Tuesday for a hamburger today.' The company that owned Lyon's Corner houses bought the Wimpy franchise, and we saw our first Wimpy bar in 1954 in London. It was not until the 1970s, however, that the franchise spread nationwide. The burgers were cooked when you ordered them and there were benders surrounding the burger (huge frankfurters). Oh, it was all so exciting at the time, and so American, just like in the movies! The Wimpy restaurant in the picture was opened on 27 July 1961, and was the first in the West Country. The countless franchise restaurants in the South West have all now gone, but the Penzance restaurant is still there, serving many of the meals it did in 1961!

The coming of the out-of-town supermarket and the home freezer suddenly made cooking all too easy and far too convenient. As you had gone out of your way to get to the supermarket, it seemed ridiculous not to get everything you needed for the whole week while you were there. Before the supermarkets came, you would decide what you wanted every day and go to get it from the local shops. The shopping trolley soon replaced the basket, as people were buying so much in one go. You had to imagine what you wanted every day in advance, and there were those displays of sticky doughnuts and ready-made meals that made it all so easy to slip into the habit of buying far too much food. The easy access to sugary pre-packaged foods has really led to our obesity problems today.

There were other influences on the British post war diet that came in the 1950s, with the first Caribbean immigrants arriving into Britain to fill the posts needed in the transport industry and the new health service. Yet their Caribbean food did not really take off during that time. It was not until the mid-1960s – when the Chinese immigrants from Hong Kong promoted their cuisine by setting up Chinese restaurants on every high street – that freshly made exotic foods were available in Britain. Then, in the 1970s, with the expulsion of Ugandan Asians by Uganda's President, Idi Amin, our old love of Indian food could be rekindled as Indian restaurants spread throughout all the major cities in Britain, competing, as they do now, with the Chinese restaurants for that Saturday night meal in town.

Here are some real post war recipes, perfect both for every day and for entertaining – just the thing for that retro party! Below is the classic special dinner party menu of the time.

Penzance Wimpy

A Wimpy classic meal. We ordered this and asked for it all to be served at once for a picture. The staff thought we were some sort of quality control group from head office! They were very relieved when I told them it was for my book

The Original Prawn Cocktail

Everybody's favourite starter in the 1960s and 1970s.

1 lettuce
225 g shelled prawns
4 tbsp mayonnaise
4 tbsp tomato sauce
A dash of Worcestershire sauce
A pinch of cayenne pepper
Salt and pepper
Brown bread and butter with crusts taken off
4 lemon slices

Method

1. Shred the lettuce and pile into the bases of tall glasses.
2. Divide the prawns among the glasses, saving 4 heads for decoration (or just 4 prawns, if you have bought them ready peeled).
3. Mix the mayonnaise, tomato sauce, Worcestershire sauce, cayenne pepper, salt and pepper together.
4. Divide this between the glasses and pour over the top of the prawns.
5. Garnish each glass with a prawn and a slice of lemon and serve the glasses on saucers with brown bread and butter triangle slices.

Duck a l'Orange

2¼ kg duck
1 level tbsp flour
Coarsely grated rind and juice of 2 medium oranges
2 tbsp dry red wine
2 tbsp redcurrant jelly
½ wine glass of sherry
Seasoning to taste

Garnish

2 thinly sliced oranges
Watercress

Method

1. Roast the duck for the required amount of time (see label on the packaging).
2. Transfer to a warm platter and keep hot.
3. Pour on all but 1 tbsp of the fat from the roast-ing tin (keep the rest of the fat for cooking later).
4. Put the roasting tin over a low heat and stir in the flour.
5. Cook for 2 minutes without browning.
6. Add the orange rind, juice, wine, jelly and sherry and cook gently until the jelly dissolves and the sauce thickens, stirring all the time.
7. Pour over the duck and garnish with orange slices and watercress.

Black Forest Gateau

200 g plain chocolate
2 tbsp milk
200 g unsalted butter
220 g caster sugar
75 g flour
A pinch of salt
4 eggs separated

Filling

300 ml double cream
225 g black cherry jam or canned cherries, drained
15 g plain chocolate, scraped or grated

Method

1. Put the chocolate in a heatproof bowl and add the milk. Place over a pan of simmering water to melt the chocolate.
2. Remove the bowl from the heat and beat in the butter, then the sugar. Continue to beat until the mixture becomes pale.
3. Beat in the flour and salt, and the egg yolks one at a time.
4. Beat the egg whites until stiff and gently fold into the mixture.
5. Butter a 20 cm loose-bottomed cake tin and put in a preheated hot oven for 40 minutes or until a skewer comes out clean when inserted in the cake.
6. Turn onto a wire rack and when cold, cut the cake into three layers.
7. Spread on the bottom layer half the jam or cherries.
8. Whip the cream lightly and spread a third of the cream over the cherries.

Dry Martini and Gin and Italian cocktail. My mother called the Italian cocktail 'gin and it'. I only drink it at Christmas and always think of my mother when I do

9. Repeat with the second layer and put the rest of the cream on top of the cake.

10. Pipe rosettes of cream around the top edge of the cake and place a preserved cherry on top of each rosette.

11. Sprinkle the grated chocolate over the cream in the centre.

Gaelic Coffee

The perfect finish to any special meal in the 1960s.

3 dessertspoons of whisky

1 level tbsp light brown sugar

Fresh strong coffee

Double cream

Method

1. Heat a stemmed wineglass with hot water and dry quickly (if you are not sure about the glass, find a thick one).

2. Pour the whiskey into the glass and stir in the sugar.

3. Pour in the coffee, leaving an inch below the rim, and keep stirring until the sugar has dissolved.

4. Pour the cream over the back of a teaspoon so that it floats on the surface to a depth of about an inch.

NB. A must have with the coffee is a dish of the new and very elegant After Eight Mints, as advertised on TV!

THE COCKTAIL PARTY

The 1960s was the era of the themed party: they had coffee parties, tea parties, spaghetti parties, cheese and wine parties, buffet parties, pancake parties, fondue parties and, of course,

Cocktail party nibbles. We all remember the essential upturned melon with lots of little sticks of cheese and pineapple on them. Why not have a retro party and enjoy them again?

the cocktail party for the more sophisticated gathering.

Dry Martini

Bond always had his with vodka, but gin was the original recipe.

1 part gin, 2 parts extra dry martini, crushed ice and decorated with a green olive.

White lady

2 parts gin, 1 part lemon juice and 1 part Cointreau, put into a cocktail shaker with crushed ice.

Daiquiri

2 parts Bacardi rum, 1 part lime juice, a dash of Angostura Bitters and ice.

Gin and Italian

Or, as my mother called it, Gin and It!

1 part gin, 2 parts sweet red vermouth and ice, topped with a maraschino cherry.

Gin and Tonic

You couldn't have a cocktail party without this one!

1 part gin, three parts tonic water, ice and a slice of lemon or lime.

Nibbles

Bowls of olives, crisps, cheese biscuits, cocktail onions and cocktail gherkins were served. Also popular was the classic melon, cut in half and covered in cocktail sticks with various nibbles attached: cheese and pineapple, cheese and cocktail onions, melon cube and prawns, melon and Parma ham, radish roses piped with cream cheese and small frankfurter sausages. Trays of little shapes of toasted bread were also served, with combinations of the following on top: prawns and mayonnaise, liver pate and rings of gherkin, smoked salmon and cream cheese, and hard-boiled egg slices with anchovy fillets curled on top. Trays of tiny sandwiches would also have been served, no more than 4 cm in diameter and, of course, the cream cheese and asparagus pinwheels were a must! These were made by cutting the crusts off white bread and rolling it so that it was very thin. The bread was then spread with butter, cream cheese and seasoning. Across one side of the bread was placed a line of tinned asparagus spears, and the whole thing was then rolled up before being sliced into rings.

THE FONDUE PARTY

Another typical party of the 1960s was the fondue party. It originally became popular when people came back from winter sports holidays in Austria. A fondue set seemed to have been one of the most popular wedding presents at the time too, but I wonder how many people actually used them on a regular basis. This is the classic cheese fondue recipe, if you happen to have a set at home, or spot one at a local car boot sale!

Cheese Fondue
450 g Gruyere cheese, grated
300 ml dry white wine
2 tsp corn flour (this prevents the cheese from curdling)
Seasoning
1 tbsp brandy
Method
1. Butter the bottom and sides of an earthenware casserole and add the cheese, seasoning and white wine mixed with the corn flour.

2. Heat slowly, stirring all the time, and add the brandy.
3. Transfer it into your fondue pot and light the candle underneath.
4. Offer your guests soft white bread cubes and toasted bread cubes to dunk.
NB. It is actually very tasty, and still a fun way to enjoy an evening with friends.

THE BUFFET PARTY

Eggs mimosa was sometimes served as a starter, but it was also a good buffet dish. An alternative egg dish was curried eggs, which I absolutely love. I serve them at most buffet parties – the perfect excuse to make them! They are very 1950s, and apparently still incredibly popular in New Zealand.

Eggs Mimosa
4 hard-boiled eggs
125 g frozen prawns
300 ml mayonnaise
Watercress to garnish
Method
1. Slice the eggs lengthwise and take out the yolks.
2. Sieve two thirds of the egg yolk into a basin and with a folk add the prawns and a little of the mayonnaise to bind them together. Stir with a fork.
3. Spoon the mixture back into the egg whites and arrange on a dish. Cover with the remaining mayonnaise.
4. Sieve the remaining egg yolk over the eggs and serve with a watercress garnish.

Curried Eggs
4 hard-boiled eggs
3 tbsp mayonnaise
1 tsp curry powder
1 tbsp chutney (like Branston pickle)
1 tsp paprika

Curried eggs. I still make these for parties and I transform any leftovers into a curried egg sandwich the next day. I think I like them best that way too

Method

1. Slice the eggs lengthwise and take out the yolks.

2. Mash the yolks with the chutney, curry powder and the mayonnaise.

3. Fill the egg whites with the mixture and arrange on a dish. Sprinkle with paprika and serve.

NB. They are well worth a try if you like eggs, and also pretty good the next day chopped up as a sandwich filling!

Devils on Horseback

Another delicious treat – not seen very often today, but still really tasty. Personally, I don't think the fried bread really adds anything to the recipe.

Cooked prunes (or ready to eat prunes)

Streaky bacon

Grated cheddar cheese

Fried bread

Method

1. Remove the stone from the prune and stuff with grated cheese.

2. Roll streaky bacon round the prune and secure with a cocktail stick.

3. Put on a baking tray and cook for 10 minutes until the bacon is brown.

4. At the same time, spread fingers of bread with dripping or cooking fat and put on a tray in the oven.

5. Serve each prune on a finger of fried bread.

Danish Open Sandwiches

Open sandwiches were very popular at buffet meals in the 1970s. Each slice of bread should be buttered and covered with lettuce before putting on a selection of the following toppings:

Devils on horseback. These are best served hot and are very tasty, but I don't know where the devil bit of the name comes from!

Scrambled egg and smoked salmon

Rings of Danish salami topped with cottage cheese and sprinkled with chives

Cottage cheese and a slice of tinned peach

A slice of beef topped with horseradish sauce

A slice of pork with applesauce

Liver pate and sliced gherkins

Blue cheese topped with a little mayonnaise and onion rings

Cottage cheese, walnuts and apple slices

Scrambled egg and a crisscross of anchovy fillets

Tinned tuna mixed with mayonnaise and sweet corn

Sliced ham topped with potato salad and sprinkled with chives

Sliced hard-boiled egg with a teaspoonful of Lumpfisk caviar on top (available in most supermarkets)

NB. These sandwiches would also be decorated with garnishes of all kinds, and were the size of a quarter of a slice of bread, cut into either triangles or squares.

MAIN MEALS

Beef Bourguignon

175 g streaky bacon

40 g lard

1 kg steak, cut into cubes

2 tbsp flour

300 ml burgundy or full bodied red wine

150 ml beef stock

450 g baby carrots, scraped and left whole

Salt and pepper

12 small onions, blanched and peeled whole

225 g button mushrooms

2 tbsp fresh parsley, finely chopped

Method

1. Fry the bacon in the fat until nice and crispy.

2. Put the bacon in the casserole. Add the meat to the pan and brown on all sides.

3. Add the beef to the casserole dish and sprinkle the flour in the pan. Stir until it browns.

4. Put the stock and wine in the pan and bring to the boil. Then pour over the meat.

5. Add the rest of the ingredients apart from the onions and mushrooms and cover the casserole. Place in a preheated moderate oven for 1½ hours.

6. Add the onions and mushrooms and put back in the oven for another 30 minutes until the onions are tender.

7. Adjust the seasoning if necessary and put into a dish. Sprinkle with the parsley and serve with new potatoes.

Mixed Grill

A variety of the following meats: Steak, lamb chops, kidney, sausage, liver

225 g tomatoes halved

225 g mushrooms (button)

Watercress to garnish

Game chips (see below)

Method

1. Grill the meats that require the longest cooking time first, and then gradually add the other meats.

2. Grill the tomato halves and toss the mushrooms in a pan of melted butter, seasoned with salt and pepper.

3. For the game chips, peel potatoes and cut into thin slices (using a potato peeler). Soak in cold water, dry thoroughly and fry in deep fat until golden brown.

4. Serve the meat on an oblong plate with the mushrooms and tomatoes and garnish with watercress, placing the game chips to one side.

Trout Almandine

4 medium-sized trout

4 tbsp flour

½ tsp salt

100 g butter

2 tsp olive oil

75 g flaked almonds

100 g peeled prawns

1 tbsp parsley

Method

1. Wash the trout and dry with kitchen paper.

2. Mix the flour with the salt and dust over the fish.

3. Fry the fish in oil and 75 g of the butter in a pan until cooked and golden on both sides.

4. Add the remaining butter to the pan and on a low heat cook the almonds until they are golden.

5. Toss in the prawns and heat through.

6. Pour the prawn and almond butter onto the fish on a plate and sprinkle with parsley. Serve with sauté potatoes and peas.

Chicken Tikka Masala

This is a very British dish now. It is thought to have been invented in a Bangladeshi restaurant in Glasgow in the 1960s when a customer said that the chicken tikka was too dry, and asked to have some gravy with it. The chef is then said to have devised a sauce out of tomato soup, yoghurt and spices for him. Whether this account is true or not, we know that the dish was invented in order to adapt an Indian dish to suit the British palate.

Marinade

300 g skinned and boned chicken breast

3 tbsp yoghurt

1 tsp lemon juice

1 tsp turmeric

1 tsp coriander

2 tsp cumin

½ tsp ginger

1 garlic clove, crushed

1 tsp salt

Tikka masala paste

1 onion, chopped finely

1 piece fresh ginger

Chicken Tikka Masala. I had my son and his girlfriend to dinner when I tried this out and they said it was the best one they had ever had

2 cloves garlic

3 tbsp olive oil

½ tsp chilli powder

4 tbsp tomato purée

1 tsp salt

4 tbsp double cream

1 bunch of fresh coriander

Method

1. Mix all the marinade ingredients together and coat the chicken. Leave in the fridge overnight.

2. In a pan, fry the onion in the oil over a slow heat until it is cooked and turning brown.

3. Add the ginger, garlic and spices and cook in the oil for 1 minute.

4. Stir in the tomato paste and stir continuously for 2 minutes.

5. Add the marinated chicken and cook for 15 minutes over a medium heat with the lid on.

6. Add the cream and stir for another 3 minutes.

7. Serve at once with white boiled rice and sprinkle with chopped fresh coriander leaves.

DESSERTS

Pear Conde

You never see this anymore, but it was everywhere in the 1960s, especially in canteen buffets as I remember. It really is very nice though, so try it!

4 cooking pears

600 ml milk

50 g pudding rice

1 tbsp sugar

2 tbsp water

1 tbsp powdered gelatine

4 tbsp red jam (no pips)

Pear Conde – every canteen used to serve these. They are very nice but maybe we have lost our taste for cold rice pudding

Method

1. Peel and cut the pears in half and core them. Stew in water until tender.
2. Cook the rice, milk and sugar in a double saucepan until creamy.
3. Soak the gelatine in 2 tsp of water and boil the jam in the remaining water. Then add to the soaked gelatine.
4. Place a spoonful of cold rice pudding in the bottom of a glass.
5. Arrange two pear halves on top.
6. When the jam mixture is cool and syrupy, pour gently over the pears and chill before serving.

Blackcurrant Pie

This is a pie you never see anymore, but it is really delicious. You will need to go to a fruit farm for the blackcurrants if you don't have your own bushes, because they don't sell them fresh in the shops any more,

225 g rich short crust pastry (see below)
1 kg blackcurrants
124 g sugar
Caster sugar

Method

1. Make the pastry and line a pie dish with it.
2. Pick over the fruit to check there are no bits of stem or mould and put half in the pie dish.
3. Sprinkle half the sugar over the currants. Then put the rest of the currants in and top with the remaining sugar.
4. Put a pastry lid on and brush with beaten egg white and caster sugar to glaze it.
5. Bake in a moderate oven for 40 minutes.

Baked Apple Dumplings

I made these in Domestic Science class and remember nibbling them on the way home as

I carried them in a basket topped with a gingham tablecloth. There was not much left of one of them by the time I got home either! They are incredibly simple to make, but so delicious. Hanna Glasse in the eighteenth century had a recipe for apple dumplings, in which the pastry case for the apple was put into individual pudding cloths and boiled in water, rather than baking it. But I tend to think that baking is nicer.

4 large cooking apples

50 g butter

50 g brown sugar

50 g raisins or currants

½ tsp cinnamon

225 g rich short crust pastry (see below)

Method

1. Peel and core the apples.

2. Mix together the melted butter, sugar, raisins and cinnamon.

3. Stuff the mixture into the cavities of the apples.

4. Roll out the pastry into 4 big circles (use a dinner plate as a cutter).

5. Sit each apple in the middle of the pastry circle, pull it up and dampen the end to make a good seal.

6. Bake in a slow oven for 1½ hours. Enjoy!

Rich Short Crust Pastry

225 g flour

150 g fat (75 g butter and 50 g lard)

A pinch of salt

25 g caster sugar

1 egg

Method

1. Sieve flour and salt into a bowl and rub in the fat until it is like fine breadcrumbs.

2. Add sugar and bind together with enough egg to make a stiff paste.

3. Put in the fridge for 1 hour before use.

Upside Down Pineapple Cake

I remember seeing Fanny Cradock do this on a TV show in black and white, and it still looked good enough to eat! My mother used to make it for special family dinners.

Base

50 g butter

50 g caster sugar

1 tin pineapple rings

1 jar maraschino cherries

Cake

125 g butter

125 g sugar

150 g plain flour

1 rounded tsp baking powder

2 eggs

1 tsp vanilla essence

Method

1. Cream the butter and sugar together and spread it at the bottom of a round ovenproof dish.

2. Drain and dry the pineapple rings and arrange them on the dish. Make half moons around the edge and a circle in the middle, putting a cherry in the middle of each half moon and one in the centre.

3. Cream the butter and sugar and then beat in the eggs and vanilla essence.

4. Mix the baking powder and flour together and fold this into the egg mixture with a metal spoon.

5. Pour this mixture over the pineapples and cherries.

6. Bake in a moderate oven for 35–40 minutes until golden.

7. Turn out onto a plate to be seen in all its caramelised base glory!

Please note that I am not including a Christmas section for the post war period because it would only contain more or less the same recipes that we use today.

❧ So what *is* British food? ❧

While researching this historic culinary journey, I have found an incredible number of foodstuffs that have been integrated into the British diet from abroad. Although this was primarily due to the culinary influences from around the globe during the dominance of the British Empire, as you have seen, it goes much farther back than that, to the foods brought over to our shores after the Roman invasion. It is strange how much we love spicy food in this country today when our climate produces none of the necessary ingredients. We really took to the spicy foods imported by the Romans from the East, but reverted back to simplistic, plain food during the Saxon and Viking periods. Spicy foods clearly didn't enthuse the Vikings, even though they travelled abroad to just as many places as the Romans. They continued to eat the traditional, plain, high protein foods that characterise the Scandinavian diet today. Our love of spicy food was renewed after the Crusaders had spent time in the Holy Land.

We seem to have had an amazing ability when confronted with completely alien culinary practices to take them to our hearts and adopt them as our own. Britain really invented fusion food, and we have been doing it for over 2,000 years. No doubt we will continue to do so well into the future.

I thought it was fascinating that the fig and walnut cakes Apicius wrote about in the Roman period were still being made in more or less the same way during the Medieval period. Today, the barbeque represents a link with our prehistoric cooking practices in that it fulfils an ancient desire to cook outdoors. Even though the wood fire was replaced by charcoal (and most recently the gas barbeque), we still love to eat hot meat with our fingers under the stars. Some of my friends tell me that one of the most depressing things about a wet summer is the fact they can't have any barbeques in the evenings. Some even ignore the weather by buying flimsy gazebos so that they can continue their habitual meaty feasts outdoors, no matter what the weather!

Who would have thought that the Romans were making pork and leek sausages 2,000 years ago! It was a real revelation to me when I read Apicius's recipe for those sausages. I thought they were invented in the twenty-first century as a fancy alternative to the normal British sausage, along with venison and pork and apple sausages. In much the same way, the almond stuffed dates I bought from my local supermarket last Christmas are just a simplified version of the recipe for Dates Alexandrine.

Knowledge of Islamic cooking methods changed our habit of dropping meat into boiling water. Instead, we now sear it in fat first, and this has really improved the flavour of our gravy. Eating lamb with mint and flavouring our sugar with vanilla pods seems so very British, but these ideas also have their roots in the Middle East. I had always assumed that sweet and sour sauce was a Chinese influence, but that too was in the Baghdad manuscript.

The Medieval type of highly spiced, sweet, yet savoury foods has gone out of favour with us today, but there are still a few long standing traditions we retain from that period, such as spiced pears in red wine and cherry clafouti/clafoutis, which I have always been led to believe was a nineteenth-century French dish.

The Elizabethans ate syllabub and rice pudding, and the origins of our modern Christmas pudding also came from this period in history, along with the recipe for brandy butter. We see the first recipe for turkey dinner with pigs in blankets (sausages wrapped in bacon) during the seventeenth century, by the eighteenth century had added a sage and onion stuffing to our traditional Christmas dinner. We also acquired a love of Welsh Rarebit recipes and toasted cheese in general.

The author

The Georgian period gave us many popular modern recipes: the sandwich and the pork and apple pie to name but a few. The recipe for apple pie with custard inside it was interesting to see, as I had always thought that Mr Kipling invented that! Our Christmas dinners also improved during this period, with the addition of chestnut stuffing, bread sauce, cranberry sauce, gravy and buttered vegetables.

The Victorians, apart from their love of curries, gave us basic kitchen cupboard items such as chutneys and brown, tomato and Worcestershire sauces. They also invented the fondue party that most of us think of as a 1970s' fashion. We still make the Victoria sandwich cake to the same weight of an egg recipe, although we make it into a round cake rather than rectangular fingers.

Recipes from the Second World War have been more or less abandoned by the cooks of Britain today, apart from maybe bubble and squeak, to which we add potatoes. Perhaps this is because war-time cooking was determined by the availability of various foods, rather than our preferences – it is not surprising, therefore, that we don't wish to eat these dishes today. Having said that, though dried eggs did enjoy a bit of a revival during the salmonella scare of the late 1980s, and if you look at the recipes included in this section, you will see that, apart from being very economical, many of them were actually very tasty too. Perhaps during these years of the so-called credit crunch, it might be the right time to take another look at them.

The food of the 1970s has made a bit of a comeback lately, as everything retro has suddenly became fashionable. As a result, great recipes like prawn cocktail, duck a l'orange and black forest gateau are being cooked in our kitchens again. The one recipe from the 1970s that is still one of the most popular meals in Britain today is the chicken tikka masala, as a recent *Britain's Best Meal* TV programme demonstrated.

They say that fusion cuisine is the latest thing, and perhaps this is true elsewhere around the globe, but in the case of our small island, fusion cuisine has characterised our cooking practices for hundreds and hundreds of years.

I hope you have enjoyed reading this book – I have certainly enjoyed writing it!

Bibliography

Apicus, *The Roman Cookery of Apicius*, translated and adapted by John Edwards (London: Random House, 1984)

Armesto, Felipe Fernandez, *Food: A History* (London: Macmillan Ltd, 2001)

Beeton, Mrs, *Mrs Beeton's Book of Household Management*, a first edition facsimile (London: Jonathan Cape Ltd, 1974)

Berriedale-Johnson, Michelle, *The British Museum Cook Book* (London: British Museum Press, 1987)

Black, Maggie, *The Mediaeval Cook Book* (London: British Museum Press, 1993)

Drummond, J.C. and Wilbraham, Anne, *The Englishman's Food* (London: Pimlico Ltd, 1939)

Flavel, Sidney, *Menus and Recipes: Cooking the Flavel Way* (London: Sidney Flavel & Co Ltd, 1962)

Glasse, Hanna, *The Art of Cookery Made Easy,* facsimile edition by Karen Hess (Massachusetts: Applewood Books, 1997)

Hammond, P.W., *Food and Feast in Mediaeval England* (Stroud: Sutton Publishing, 1998)

Isitt, Verity, *Take a Buttock of Beef* (Southampton: Ashford Press Publishing, 1987)

Mckendry, Maxime, *Seven Centuries of English Cooking* (London: C. Tinling & Co Ltd, 1973)

Moss, Peter, *Meals Through The Ages* (London: George G. Harrop Ltd, 1958)

Pegge, Samuel (compiler), *The Forme of Cury* (Bibliobazaar Ltd, 2006)

Price, Rebecca, *The Compleat Cook or the Secrets of a Seventeenth-Century Housewife,* compiled by Madeleine Masson (London: Routledge & Kegan Paul Ltd, 1974)

Ray, Elizabeth (compiler), *The Best of Eliza Acton* (Southampton: The Camelot Press Ltd, 1968)

Sass, Lorna, *To the Queen's Taste: Elizabethan Feasts and Recipes* (London: John Murray Ltd, 1976)

Sim, Alison, *Food and Feasting in Tudor England* (Stroud: Sutton Publishing, 1997)

Spurling, Hilary, *Elizor Fettiplaces Receipt Book* (Middlesex: Penguin Books Ltd, 1987)

❦ Index ❦

A dish of Spiced Peaches 28
A dish of Spiced Pears 28
A dish of Snow 72
A fancy dish of Herrings 94
Almond Hedgehog
Almond Milk 46
Almond Milk Fruit Pie 51
Anzac Biscuits 135
Apple and Custard Pie 95
Apple Fritters 95
Apples in Red Jelly 108
Apricot Ice Cream 97
Apricot relish 29
Asparagus Omelette 89
Asparagus Toasted Cheese 79
Aunty Rye's Long Biscuit
    Cream 85

Bacon and Potatoes 126
Bacon Toasted Cheese 79
Baked Apple Dumplings 152
Baked Carrot Pudding 84
Baked Fruit Pudding 135
Barley Drink 28
Barley Gruel 40
Battered Celery Hearts 90
Beef and Lettuce Salad and
    mustard 129
Beef Bourguignon 149
Beef Pinwheels 149
Beef Stew 91
Beef Stew a la mode 105
Beef Stew a la mode economi-
    cal 105
Beef Stew without fruit 61

Beetroot Pancakes 90
Bengal Mango Chutney 116
Bermuda Witches 106
Black Forest Gateau 144
Blackberry and plum crumble
    40
Blackcurrant Pie 152
Boiled Beef and Carrots 105
Boiled Chicken with Orange
    62
Boiled Egg and Anchovy 21
Boiled Pigeon with rice cream
Boiled Rabbit with Stuffing
    61
Brawn 69
Brawn 119
Bread Baked in Honey 16
Bread Cup fillings:
    Bacon Leek and Thyme 14
    Fried Crab Apple and
        Honey 16
    Hazel nut and Berry 15
    Plum and Honey and
        Venison 14
    Sea Beet, curd and egg 16
    Smoked Fish, Leek and
        Nuts 14
Bread Pudding 51
Bread Salad 21
Bread Sauce 83
Bread Sauce (Georgian) 98
Breaded Ham 93
Breast of Lamb with Peas 105
Brie Tart 42
Brillat Savarin's Fondue 103

Brown Stew and Dumplings
    126
Bubble and Squeak 103
Burdock Roots Bake 76

Cabbage Stew 48
Candied Peel 46
Candied Suckets 71
Chantilly Basket 108
Cheese Fondue 147
Cheese Pudding 132
Cheese sandwich (toasted) 123
Cherry Pottage 64
Cherry Pudding 52
Cheshire Pork Pie 93
Chestnut Stuffing 97
Chicken Tikka Marsala 150
Christmas cake with Icing 99
Christmas Cake 86
Christmas Cake (modest) 87
Christmas Cake (without eggs)
    137
Christmas Fruit Snow 138
Christmas Mustard Pickle 84
Christmas Plum Pudding 70
Christmas Pudding Aunt
    Francklines 85
Christmas Pudding Mrs
    Beeton's 143
Cider Syllabub 80
Cocktail Party 145
Coconut Soup 115
Corned Beef Hash 130
Corned Beef Rissoles 130
Creamed Sardine Pie 130

Cresses 43
Crisp Butter Cake 71
Crumb Fudge 138
Cucumber Pudding 59
Curried Beef 111
Curried Chicken 113
Curried Cod 113
Curried Eggs 111
Curried Eggs 1960's 147
Curry or Paprika Stew 125
Curry Powder (Mrs Beeton's)
    131
Curry Powder (Mr Arnott's)
    111

Daiquiri 146
Danish Open Sandwiches 148
Date and Herb Sauce for Tuna
    26
Dates Alexandrine 32
Delhi Pudding 117
Devils on Horseback 148
Diet Bread 81
Dresden Patties 132
Dry Martini 146
Duck a l'Orange 144
Duke of Buckingham's
    Pudding with Sherry Sauce
    99

Eighteenth-century North of
    England Festive Pie 98
Eggs Mimosa 147
English Rarebit 91

Fairy Butter 95
Fine Crisp Butter Cake 64
Fish Cakes 131
Fish Curry 131
Fish Pasties 131
Floating Islands 100
Fried Beans and Onions 85
Fried Fig Tarts 43
Fried Herbs 52
Fried Rock Samphire 9
Fried Whiting and Apple Sauce
    63

Frosted Holly leaves 121
Frumente 47
Frumenty 40

Gaelic Coffee 145
Gin and Italian 146
Gin and Tonic 146
Ginger Cream Tart 70
Gingerbread 81
Gode Broth 47
Gode Paest 41
Gode Powder 47
Grand Mince Pie (Savoury) 68

Ham (cold) 30
Hamburgers in Brown Sauce
    128
Hard Boiled Eggs in Mustard
    Sauce 60
Hard Sauce 70
Herb Stuffing for Turkey 66
Herby Pie 76
Herring Pye 78
Honey Drinks 14
Honey Omelette 25
Hot Beetroot 25
Hot Christmas Punch 121
Hot Water Crust Pastry 68
    & 94

Icing for Christmas Cake 99
Indian Fritters 117
Indian Pickle 116
Indian Trifle 117

Kedgeree 112
Knot Biscuits 81

Lady How's Little Plum
    Puddings 84
Lady How's Pease Pottage 75
Lady Sheldon's gravy for Pork
    78
Lamb boiled with green grass 6
Lamb Chop Hot Pot 127
Lamb Stew 6
Lamb Stew with Mint and

Apples 34
Lamb Stew with mint and
    spices 34
Lark Pie 104
Lark, Sparrow, Blackbird and
    Woodcock (Bake) 77
Leeches Christmas Broth 82
Leche Lumbard or Date Slices
    50
Lemon Cream 81
Lemon Fromage 126
Liver Pate 62

Macaroni Cheese 103
Macaroni Cheese Wartime 130
Manchester Pudding 107
Mango Chutney 138
Marchpane 71
Meat Curry 127
Meaty Dumplings 77
Medieval dish of chickpeas 48
Mince in the Hole 128
Mince Pie 100
Mincemeat 99
Mincemeat Mrs Beeton's 145
Ministry of Food Christmas
    Pudding 137
Ministry of Food Curried
    Corned Beef Balls 30
Ministry of Food Mincemeat
    138
Ministry Mock Icing for
    Christmas cake 138
Minted Mackerel and sorrel
    sauce 49
Mixed Grill 150
Mock Goose (Country Style)
    136
Mock Rum Cream for Mince
    Pies 136
Mr Arnott's Currie 111
Mrs Beeton's unrivalled
    Christmas Cake 119
Mrs Beeton's Mincemeat 121
Mrs Lord's Hash recipe 78
Mrs Whitehead's stew of rump
    beef 77